Love
Food

Published by Blink Publishing

3.25, The Plaza,

535 Kings Road,

Chelsea Harbour,

London, SW10 0SZ

www.blinkpublishing.co.uk

facebook.com/blinkpublishing

twitter.com/blinkpublishing

978–1–910536–61–2

A CIP catalogue of this book is available from the British Library.

Design by Steve Leard
leard.co.uk

Printed and bound in Italy

1 3 5 7 9 10 8 6 4 2

Papers used by Blink Publishing are natural, recyclable products made from wood grown in sustainable forests. The manufacturing processes conform to the environmental regulations of the country of origin.

Blink Publishing is an imprint of the Bonnier Publishing Group
www.bonnierpublishing.co.uk

Love
Food

Josie Gibson

BLINK
bringing you closer

Contents

I have worked many hours writing this book and testing recipes. Me being permanently busy has placed a strain on most of my friendships and I'd like to thank them for sticking with me.

I would like to dedicate this book to two people. My bestie Mia Williams, who has suffered such loss and tragedy this year but still remains positive, full of life and energy, and makes me laugh virtually every day. The second is Denise Lansdowne who gave up some weekends that she could have spent with her beautiful family to work with me. Thanks for the giggles and all your help.

Josie.

Introduction

Losing six stone is without a doubt the most emotional journey I've ever been on and the biggest achievement of my life. Having struggled with obesity for two decades, I want to help others who, like me, have spent too many years looking at a reflection they hate.

Throughout my teens and twenties I tried every diet under the sun to get the body I wanted. Nothing worked and if it did, the weight would pile right back on afterwards. After leaving the *Big Brother* house as a size 20 at just 25-years-old, I decided that something needed to change. I was constantly being asked about my weight in interviews: Was I planning to lose it? Why didn't I want to do a bikini shoot? How was I so confident when I was the fattest *Big Brother* winner ever?

I needed to take drastic action. So I hit the books, took up personal training and advanced nutritional advisor courses and eventually became a personal trainer and nutritional advisor. I started to identify what was keeping me (and others) big. I began to realise that I had been battling an addiction to sugar and processed foods. The majority of foods that I had been buying from the supermarket (even those that were supposed to be healthy) were crammed with extortionate amounts of sugar and salt in order to make them palatable. 'Hidden' sugars are in nearly every processed food you can buy – so I cut myself off from processed foods.

Even after a week of clean eating I was shocked by the outcome. Not only was the weight dropping off – but my skin looked luminous. The hunger pangs that plagued me on every other diet disappeared; my mood swings that had ruined relationships seemed a distant memory; my eyes were brighter, and my dark circles were gone. I felt like I had a newfound energy and was on my way to a new lease of life. All my life (well since the age of 6!) I'd wanted to just be a normal-sized person and now it was finally happening!

After finding the one diet that actually worked, I was so inspired to share it. I sought out pioneering scientist Rob Corney from Loughborough University to help me build a structured diet formula based on my weight loss for others so that they could finally win their battles with fat too. With Rob's expertise and my experience, we created the most effective formula for weight loss. We developed and tested the formula for an entire year to make sure that it is perfect. I then created the Slimmables website to make it easy to follow.

Joining Slimmables isn't about depriving yourself. It's not about starving yourself or a quick fix before you pile it all back on again. It's about making a change. About making the right health choices for you. It's a lifestyle plan that will see you finally reach the weight you've always wanted to be and maintain it for life. I don't see Slimmables as a 'diet'; Slimmables is simply eating normally, instead of being on a diet of processed foods and excessive sugars.

Now we all know calorie counting diets don't really work. A study conducted by obesity researcher Zoe Harcombe reported that 'despite the UK National Food Survey confirming that we ended the last century eating 25 per cent fewer calories than in the 1970s, the obesity rate has increased six-fold since then.' I completely agree (although on Slimmables we use a calorie currency simply as a guide to portion control). It's not how much we are eating; it's the types of food that we are eating that cause the problem.

Based on this principle, the only ingredients required for the recipes in this book are what I call Clean and Green ingredients – fruits and vegetables we are designed to eat and are naturaly grown for human consumption, and meat and fish which would have been hunted by our caveman ancestors. The human body was not designed to eat hydrogenated oils or food laced with chemicals and refined sugar (the most socially addictive drug in the world). When you eat a food that is tampered with and contains lots of chemicals that your body can not break down, it simply converts it to fat or makes you sick. So why do we keep eating those things and wondering why we have problems with our weight and health?

So here is a list of foods that we give the Clean and Green thumbs up. All our recipes are made with entirely Clean and Green ingredients. The diet is designed so you can clean your digestion, rebalance hormones, stop insulin spikes which lead to weight gain but make you blossom into a beautiful flower (ok well maybe not a flower but a better version of yourself!).

Alongside each recipe you will find a Slimbite number and recipe rating. Slimbites are calories that are easier to count, with one Slimbite equal to 50 calories. If you are on a 1,500-calorie diet then you are looking for around 30 Slimbites a day. A note of caution: you should never starve yourself on this plan either. When you starve yourself you start to mess around with your metabolism and believe me when you start to eat again it will come back and then some!

For the ultimate weight loss try and stay under 100g of carbohydrate a day. Identify your weakness foods and simply make the healthy alternative to it. Get your whole house involved – that way it's not as easy to slip off the rails and you and your family will get healthier and happier together. You will have cravings but you need to stay strong and not cave into them. When you come through the other side you will feel incredible. Set a goal – whether that's a certain weight you want to hit or an item of clothing you want to get into: set the goal and have that goal in sight daily.

Clean & Green Foods

Vegetables	*All Herbs & Spices*	*Vegetables*	*Fruits*	*Meat*	*Oils*
Artichokes	Basil	Turnip	Acia	Chicken	Olive oil
Asparagus	Bay leaves	Carrot	Apple	Goat meat	Coconut oil
Aubergine	Black pepper	Butternut Squash	Avocado	Lamb	Rapeseed oil
Baby corn	Cayenne	Yam	Banana	Lean beef	Avocado oil
Beansprouts	Chilli	Beetroot	Blueberries	Pork	Lard
Broccoli	Chinese five spice	Parsnip	Strawberries	Rabbit	Sesame oil
Brussels sprouts	Chives	Sweet potato	Raspberries	Venison	Walnut oil
White cabbage	Cloves	Medium potato	Cantaloupe	Veal	Tahini
Red cabbage	Cinnamon	Jacket potato	Cherries	Duck	Unrefined palm oil
Savoy cabbage	Coriander	Corn on the cob	Grapefruit	Goose	Macadamia oil
Cauliflower	Cumin		Grapes	Quail	Flax Seed oil
Kale	Dill		Guava	Ostrich	Peanut oil
Celeriac	Fennel	*Peas & Beans*	Watermelon	Turkey	Almond oil
Celery	Garam masala	Kidney beans	Honeydew melon	Partridge	Beef Tallow
All chillies	Garlic	Chickpeas	Kiwi	Pigeon	Chia seed oil
Choi sum	Ginger	Blackeye beans	Lychee	Kangaroo	Hemp seed oil
Collard greens	Horseradish	Red lentils	Mango	Crocodile	Palm oil
Courgette	Lemongrass	Adzuki bean	Nectarine		Palm shortening
Cucumber	Mint	Soy bean	Orange		Chilli oil
Shallots	Mustard	Anasazi beans	Papaya	*Fish & Shellfish*	
Fennel	Nutmeg	Fava beans	Passion fruit	Cod	
French bean	Oregano seeds	Pigeon peas	Pear	Haddock	*Flours & Milk*
Garlic	Paprika	Split peas	Pineapple	Salmon	Coconut flour
Gherkins	Parsley	Broad beans	Peach	Mackerel	Almond flour
Ginger	Peppermint	Butter beans	Plum	Snapper	Sesame flour
Endive	Rosemary	Mung beans, whole	Pomegranate	Sardines	Potato starch (gluten free)
Leeks	Saffron	Pinto beans	Star fruit	Trout	Peanut flour
Lettuce (all types)	Sage		Tangerine	Tuna	Tapioca flour
Mange tout	Sea salt		Apricot	Anchovy	Teff flour
Mushroom	Star anise	*Nuts & Seeds*	Blackberries	Sea Bass	Hemp flour
Mustard greens	Tarragon	Almonds (plain)	Plantain	Carp	Flax meal
Chicory	Thyme	Brazil nuts	Dates	Catfish	Unsweetened coconut milk
Pak choi	Turmeric	Cashews	Figs	Flatfish	Unsweetened almond milk
Radishes	Vanilla pods	Wasabi peas	Bread fruit	Flounder	Unsweetened soya milk
Red onion	Stevia	Chestnuts	Currants	Grouper	Hemp milk
Runner beans		Coconut	Damson	Hake	Unsweetened hazelnut milk
Spinach		Hazelnuts	Dragon fruit	Halibut	Chickpea flour
Sugar snap peas		Mixed nuts	Egg plant	Herring	Quinoa flour
Petit pois		Peanuts	Elderberry	Monkfish	Hazelnut flour
Tomato		Pecans		Mullet	
Watercress		Pine nuts		Pike	
Bamboo		Pumpkin seeds		Perch	*Eggs*
Chard		Sunflower seeds		Plaice	Chicken egg
Heart of palm		Walnuts		Rockfish	Duck egg
Onions		Macadamia nuts		Skate	Turkey egg
Peas		Chia seeds		Sole	Quail egg
Peppers		Hemp seeds		Sunfish	Any other form of eggs
Pumpkin		Sesame seeds		Tilapia	
Split peas		Flaxseed		Turbot	
Spring onions		Pistachios		Scallops	
Swede		Quinoa		Crab	
Fennel				Oysters	*Other*
Swiss chard				Clams	Water
Pickled onion				Octopus	Coconut water
				Squid	Juiced fruit & vegetables
				Prawns	Vanilla extract
				Mussels	Apple cider vinegar
				Lobster	Raw cocoa powder
				Crayfish	Cocoa nibs
				Kippers	
				Pollock	
				Dover sole	
				Cockles	
				Scampi (Not breaded)	

Breakfast

The last decade has seen a 60% increase in diabetes. That's an increase of over one million people in the UK. Diabetes costs the NHS £10 billion a year and there is no doubt that, given this surge in diagnoses, the diabetes epidemic will bankrupt our amazing free NHS service. Why is diabetes such a problem for us? All of the signs point to the sheer number of 'contaminated' processed foods we eat. When we eat processed foods, like most breakfast cereals for instance, they quickly break down into glucose (sugar), causing our insulin levels to skyrocket while also being devoid of important vitamins and minerals. And if that's not bad enough, the vast majority of packaged breakfast foods are highly deceptive about their portion sizes and nutritional information.

Think about that. Every morning all of our poor bodies are forced to produce massive levels of insulin to deal with the processed foods that we continue to eat. Not only does this exasperate your body first thing in the morning and throw off your nutritional balance for the entire day, but it also has noticeable long-term consequences on our health, leading to type 2 diabetes and obesity (among other things).

I have been working with a marvellous woman called Cathy; she lost 8 stone eating on the Slimmables Clean and Green plan. She was reliant on medication for her type 2 diabetes, and after just seven months of a clean, good diet, she was able to come off that medication for good – and she looks like a brand new woman too! Seeing this progress in real life… seeing a disease get cured simply through eating a natural diet only further instills the overall detriment that sugar and processed foods have on our health.

People who struggle with their weight are often addicted to sugar. I know, because I was one of them. You are constantly looking for your next hit all day, every day. I've been saying this for a long time: sugar is the most socially addictive drug in the world. In fact, when most people get their 'sugar fix', they experience the same chemical reaction as people who get their fix of a hardcore stimulant such as cocaine. And what's worse – sugar is virtually everywhere. Even foods that aren't sweet (like sauces and bread) actually convert into sugar after you eat them. The only way to cut yourself off is to eat a diet that is mostly Clean and Green.

Start the morning with lots of good fats, nutrients and natural sugars that your body can easily digest without massively spiking your insulin levels. Lots of scientific research suggests it takes 21 days to make a new habit – so I've included 21 breakfast recipes so that you can make it a routine to start your day off clean!

Warming Winter Smoothie

Serves: **1**

 Slimbites: **7**

240 ml coconut milk
100 g soaked cashews (soak in water
  overnight, drain)
1 tbsp. coconut butter
1/2 tsp. vanilla powder

1/2 tsp. ground cinnamon, plus extra for sprinkling
1/2 tsp. ground cardamom
1/4 tsp. ground ginger
tiny pinch of ground cloves
tiny pinch of sea salt

♥ Blend all ingredients until smooth.

Top Tip: Serve in a bowl and eat with a spoon so its feels like you are being filled up. Full of rich, nutritious fats, this will keep you going through the winter period!

Superfood Smoothie

Serves: **2**

 Slimbites: **2.5**

240ml unsweetened almond milk
150g organic, wild fresh or frozen blueberries
50g organic fresh or frozen strawberries
1 avocado
1 tsp. organic flaxseed
1 banana

♥ In a blender, combine all ingredients. Blend
  until smooth.

1 handful organic spinach
100g coconut yoghurt
1 tbsp. chia seeds
1 scoop of power greens powder if available
4 ice cubes

Spiced Apple Warm Winter Smoothie

Serves: **2**

 Slimbites: **4**

480ml water
2 apples
1 banana
4 tbsp. dried coconut
75g dates

4 tbsp. pumpkin seeds
1/2 tsp. powdered ginger
1/4 tsp. cayenne pepper
1 tsp. vanilla extract

♥ Blend the dry ingredients and liquid first.
♥ Add fruits and the rest of the ingredients
   and blend until smooth.

Green Smoothie

Serves: **2**

♥ Slimbites: **2**

2 handfuls of spinach
3 slices of cucumber
1/2 stalk celery
1 tsp. cinnamon

3 medium strawberries
1 tbsp. flaxseed
40g blueberries
240 ml unsweetened almond milk

♥ Combine all ingredients and blend
until smooth.

Carrot and Ginger Juice

Serves: **1**

 Slimbites: **2**

4 carrots
2 apples
1 piece of ginger (about 2.5cm – you can use
    more depending on how much you love ginger)

♥ Juice all ingredients into a glass and serve.

Parsnip and Pear Juice

Serves: **1**

 Slimbites: **2**

2 apples
2 pears
1 parsnip
1/2 a lemon

♥ Using a juicer (my favourite is a Sage juicer!),
juice all ingredients to make a quick healthy
morning juice.

Apple Pancakes

Serves: **6**

 Slimbites: **5**

1 tbsp. coconut oil
2 tsp. cinnamon
4 eggs
240ml coconut milk
1–2 tbsp. date syrup
1 tsp. pure vanilla extract
8 tbsp. coconut flour
pinch of nutmeg
pinch of sea salt

For the apple topping:
2 medium apples, diced
1 tbsp. cinnamon
3 tbsp. additional coconut milk
3 tbsp. coconut oil
2 tbsp. date syrup

additional coconut oil for cooking pancakes

♥ Melt a tablespoon of coconut oil over medium heat in a frying pan.
♥ Add in the diced apples and cinnamon.
♥ Cook until apples are soft – for about 5-8 minutes.
♥ While apples are cooking, mix your pancake ingredients by combining the eggs, coconut milk, date syrup and vanilla, and then adding in coconut flour, cinnamon, nutmeg and salt.
♥ When the apples are cooked, fold half of the apple mixture into the pancake batter and stir.
♥ Add to the apples left in the frying pan, the 3 tablespoons coconut milk, coconut oil and date syrup and stir to combine. Set aside this topping until the pancakes have finished cooking.

♥ Pour the pancake batter into a well-greased frying pan turned to medium low in your desired pancake size.
♥ Once bubbles appear over the top of the pancakes, it's time to flip!
♥ Flip and continue cooking for about a minute or until both sides are golden brown.
♥ Serve with the topping

Baked Avocado

Serves: **2**

 Slimbites: **5**

1 ripe avocado
2 fresh eggs
a pinch of pepper
1/2 tbsp. chopped chives

♥ Preheat the oven to 180°C/fan 160°C/gas 4.
♥ Slice the avocado in half and take out the pit. Scoop out two tablespoons of flesh from the centre of the avocado – just enough so the egg will fit snugly in the centre.
♥ Place the avocado halves in a small baking dish. Do your best to make sure they fit tightly.
♥ Crack an egg into each avocado half. Crack the yolk in first and let the egg whites spill in to fill up the rest of the shell.

♥ Place in the oven and bake for 15 to 20 minutes (cooking time will depend on the size of your eggs and avocados). Just make sure the egg whites have enough time to set.
♥ Remove from oven and season with pepper and chives.

Smoked Salmon and Scrambled Eggs

Serves: **2**

 Slimbites: **5**

3 eggs
3 tbsp. coconut milk
4 slices smoked salmon
2 portabello mushrooms
1 tbsp. coconut oil
salt and pepper, to taste

- ♥ Preheat the oven to 180°C/fan 160°C/gas 4.
- ♥ Crack the eggs into a bowl and whisk with the coconut milk to make a basic scrambled egg mix. Season to taste and set to one side.
- ♥ Toast mushrooms on both sides in the oven for around 15 minutes.
- ♥ Melt a tablespoon of coconut oil in a non-stick saucepan and pour in the egg mixture and cook until it scrambles.
- ♥ Arrange the smoked salmon on each mushroom. Then dress with a couple of spoonfuls of the scrambled egg.

Banana Bacon Almond Butter Bites

Serves: **6**

 Slimbites: **3**

2 large bananas
1 tbsp. almond butter
2 strips of cooked crispy bacon
juice from 1 lemon (optional)

♥ Cut each strip of bacon into three pieces.
♥ Peel the bananas and cut them into three even-sized pieces.
♥ Cut each piece lengthways, like a sandwich. This will create six banana sandwich bites.
♥ Brush each banana with a little lemon juice to prevent browning.
♥ Spread almond butter on the bottom banana of each sandwich bite.
♥ Place a piece of bacon on top of the almond butter and place the banana sandwich bit back on top.
♥ Place in the refrigerator to chill before serving.

Egg Muffins

Serves: **6 egg muffins**

 Slimbites: **2**

6 eggs
1 medium white onion, chopped
1/2 medium courgette, diced small and cooked
  in microwave for approximately 30 seconds
  to soften

4 slices of bacon, cooked and crumbled
1 whole roasted red pepper, chopped
60g baby spinach leaves, chopped
1/4 tsp. sea salt
black pepper to taste

- ♥ Preheat oven to 180°C/fan 160°C/gas 4.
- ♥ Grease a muffin tin with olive oil or coconut oil.
- ♥ In a large bowl, whisk the eggs along with the
  salt and pepper. Add the remaining ingredients
  and whisk.
- ♥ Distribute mixture evenly among six cups
  and bake for around 10 minutes, checking
  occasionally, or until eggs are set in middle.
- ♥ Remove from oven and serve.

Top Tip: These muffins are perfect
for a work snack or lunch. They are
so low in Slimbites, offer virtually
no carbohydrates and are so full
of protein.

Paleo Granola

Serves: **8**

♥ Slimbites: **10**

400g mixed almonds, hazelnuts, macadamia
and Brazil nuts
100g dried fruit (plums, dried cherries,
cranberries, apricots, dates)
70g sunflower seeds

50g desiccated coconut, unsweetened
1 tbsp. vanilla extract
1 tbsp. coconut oil
serve with a topping of your choice

♥ Preheat oven to 165°C/fan 145°C/gas 3.
♥ Add the nuts (reserving half a cup) and the
dried fruit to a food processor. Pulse, rather
than blend, the mix ever so lightly. Some of the
ingredients will turn into a fine flour/meal-like
consistency but that's what we want – a variety
of shapes and sizes. Transfer to a large bowl.
♥ Grease a large baking tray with some coconut
oil and line it with baking paper, making sure
the sides are covered. Spoon the mix into the
tray and flatten with a spatula.
♥ Bake in three stages. First bake for about 12
minutes and then stir the mix as the top would
have browned by now. Then bake for 8–10
minutes and stir again. Finally bake for the
last 4–5 minutes.

♥ Remove and let it cool completely. The
mixture should have turned crispy and a dark,
golden brown. Serve.

*Top Tip: Keep granola fresh in an
airtight jar to use in the morning.*

Full English Breakfast

Serves: **1**

 Slimbites: **13**

2 eggs
2 sausages
2 rashers bacon

2 small tomatoes, cut in half
2 button mushrooms, cut in half
a large handful of spinach

- ♥ Place the sausages, bacon, mushrooms and tomatoes under a preheated grill with a flat plate. When the bacon is ready to turn over, crack an egg onto the grill alongside the sausages, bacon, mushrooms and tomatoes.
- ♥ When everything is cooked, place on a warm plate and add spinach to grill.
- ♥ Toss spinach so it doesn't burn.
- ♥ Serve.

Sautéed Potatoes with Bacon and Spinach

Serves: **2**

 Slimbites: **8**

2 medium sweet potatoes, peeled and diced
1 medium apple, peeled, cored and diced
2 tbsp. coconut oil
3 rashers bacon, chopped into small pieces
30g baby spinach
1/2 a medium onion, diced
salt and pepper to taste

♥ In a large non-stick frying pan, heat a
   tablespoon of coconut oil over a medium high
   heat. Once hot, add the diced sweet potatoes.
   When the sweet potatoes start to soften, add the
   onions and the bacon.
♥ Once the bacon begins to brown, add the
   diced apples and a pinch of sea salt to the pan.
♥ Cook until the apples and the potatoes
   are completely softened and the bacon is
   completely cooked.
♥ Add the spinach to the frying pan and cook
   everything for a further 1 to 2 minutes.
♥ Serve warm and with a side of your choice.

Top Tip: This is a large serving and
should keep you full until lunch...
nom nom!

Spicy Quinoa Porridge

Serves: **2**

 Slimbites: **5**

85g quinoa
240ml coconut milk
240ml water
1/2 tsp. ground cinnamon
2 pinches ground nutmeg

2 pinches ground ginger
2 pinches of salt
2 tbsp. date syrup
1/2 tsp. vanilla extract (optional)
2 tbsp. currants or raisins

♥ Place the quinoa in a fine mesh sieve and rinse well with cold water. Pour the coconut milk and water into a saucepan on a medium heat, with a pinch of cinnamon, nutmeg, ginger and salt.

♥ Add the quinoa and cook for 5 minutes, stirring until the grains are separated and smell fragant.

♥ Add another pinch of nutmeg, ginger and salt. Bring to a boil.

♥ Reduce the heat to maintain a simmer and cook uncovered, stirring occasionally, for 15 to 20 minutes, until the quinoa is tender. Remove from the heat. Stir in the date syrup and vanilla extract.

♥ Stir in the currants (or raisins). Return the cereal to the saucepan and stir over a medium-low heat for 1 to 2 minutes, until thickened slightly.

Lansdown Waffle

Serves: **8**

 Slimbites: **6**

For the waffle:
4 large eggs
1 large ripe banana
240ml full-fat coconut milk
5 tbsp. coconut oil, warmed if solid
2 tsp. vanilla extract
2 tbsp. date syrup
60g coconut flour
90g potato flour
2 tsp. ground cinnamon
1 tsp. sea salt
melted coconut oil (to grease waffle iron)

For the cinnamon syrup:
4 tbsp. coconut oil, warmed if solid
4 tbsp. date syrup
2 tsp. vanilla extract
2 tsp. ground cinnamon
sliced bananas (optional)

♥ To make waffles, combine all waffle ingredients in a blender and blend until smooth. Allow the batter to sit for about 10 minutes and then blend again for about 3 seconds before using.

♥ Coat your waffle iron with a little bit of coconut oil to prevent everything from sticking.

♥ Pour enough batter to cover the bottom of the waffle maker, close and cook until light brown.

♥ To make the cinnamon syrup, melt all topping ingredients together in a small saucepan and stir until combined. Cook until thickened.

♥ Drizzle over waffles and top with sliced bananas (optional).

Top Tip: I love a kitchen gadget! Waffle irons are cheap, quick and easy to use — they're one of my top gadgets to have in the kitchen!

Easy-peasy Omelette

Serves: **1**

♥ Slimbites: **6**

1 tbsp. coconut oil
1 medium red pepper, diced
40g button mushrooms, sliced
1 small onion, diced

2 eggs
a pinch of salt

♥ Heat the coconut oil in a frying pan over a
medium-high heat. Add the onion, fry for 2–3
minutes, then add peppers and mushrooms.
Cook for a further 5–7 minutes and place on
a plate.
♥ While mushrooms and peppers are cooking,
whisk two eggs with a pinch of salt.
♥ Pour the egg mixture into a hot frying pan
(add a little more coconut oil if dry). Swirl
the egg mixture around to form a flat, round
omelette shape. Cook for 2 minutes until just
slightly wet in the middle.
♥ Gently fold over and turn the heat off.
♥ Fold the peppers, mushrooms and onion inside
the omelette on a plate and serve.

Wheat-free Toast

Serves: **10**

 Slimbites: **6**

145g blanched almond flour
4 tbsp. flaxseed
4 tbsp. coconut oil
1 tbsp. apple cider vinegar
1 tbsp. date syrup
1/4 tsp. salt

1 tsp. gluten-free baking powder
5 eggs
2 tbsp. coconut flour
3 tbsp. golden (or brown) flaxseeds
3 tbsp. pumpkin seeds

- Preheat oven to 175°C/fan 155°C/gas 5.
- Place the eggs in a bowl and whisk.
- Add the remaining wet ingredients (date syrup, coconut oil and vinegar).
- In a separate bowl, mix together the dry ingredients (almond flour, flaxseed, baking powder, coconut flour, flaxseeds, pumpkin seeds and salt).
- Add the wet ingredients to the dry ingredients and mix well using a spoon.
- Pour batter in a lined loaf tin.
- Bake in the oven for approximately 30 minutes, or until golden.
- Cool before eating.

Pumpkin Pancakes with Bacon & Cashews

Serves: **10–12 pancakes**

 Slimbites: **4**

4 large eggs
4 tbsp. almond butter
125g pumpkin puree (my favourite is 'Libby's
    100% natural', sold in Waitrose)
60ml date syrup
60ml coconut milk
2 tbsp. melted coconut oil (plus a bit more for the pan)
1/2 tsp. vanilla extract

40g coconut flour
1 and 1/2 tsp. cinnamon
3/4 tsp. ground nutmeg
1/4 tsp. ground ginger
1/4 tsp. ground cardamom
4 tbsp. chopped cashews
1/4 tsp. sea salt
6 slices cooked bacon, chopped

♥ Preheat a griddle or shallow sauté pan on a
  medium heat. Lightly brush with coconut oil.
♥ Place all of the wet ingredients in the bowl
  of a stand mixer. Beat on medium speed
  until combined.
♥ Add the remaining dry ingredients; beat until
  smooth and fully incorporated. Allow batter
  to sit for 5 minutes and beat again for 30
  seconds until thickened.
♥ Pour 60ml of batter for each pancake onto the
  hot pan. Wait for the edges to start to
  lift, about 30 seconds, then gently flip the
  pancake over.
♥ Continue cooking for 15–20 seconds, until
  cooked through and browned on both sides.
♥ Top pancakes with the bacon pieces.

Porridge Without the Bloat

Serves: **1**

 Slimbites: **5**

120ml full fat coconut milk
60ml water
3 tbsp. coconut flour
2 tbsp. finely shredded coconut
1/2 medium banana, mashed
toppings of your choice

♥ In a small saucepan, mix together the coconut
  milk and the water, and add the coconut flour
  and shredded coconut.
♥ Bring to a boil, cover, reduce heat to low, and
  simmer for 5 minutes. Stir halfway through.
♥ Remove from the heat and whisk in the
  mashed banana. Stir briefly, then return to
  the heat and stir until thickened – for about
  2 to 3 minutes.
♥ Serve with a topping of your choice.

Cheeky Chorizo Burgers

Serves: **9–11 burgers**

 Slimbites: **5**

225g ground lean beef
225g chorizo sausage without the outer casing,
   finely chopped
2 red onions, diced
9-11 eggs
2 large red tomatoes, sliced

2 avocados, sliced
1 lime
1 tbsp. olive oil
rock salt and ground black pepper, to taste
fresh rocket (optional)

♥ Preheat the oven to 180°C/fan 160°C/gas 4.
♥ Mix the chorizo sausage with the ground beef
  in a bowl.
♥ Form 6 large round patties out of the meat,
  placing them on a greased baking tray. Season
  them with rock salt and pepper.
♥ Bake until well cooked (approximately
  20 minutes).
♥ While the burgers are baking, heat the olive
  oil in a pan over a medium heat. Add the
  onions into the pan and fry until they become
  caramelised. Push to one side of the pan.
♥ Cook the eggs in the same pan, keeping
  the yolk runny so you can use it as a sauce
  for the burgers.
♥ Place the burgers on a plate, squeezing a bit of
  lime juice over them. Top with the fried onions,
  tomato slices, avocado slices, and the fried egg.
  Serve on a bed of fresh rocket salad (optional).

Top Tip: I make around 10 burger patties, wrap each one in cling film and freeze for a later date.

Lunch

Like you and everyone else, I'm extremely busy. That's why I love to batch cook and prepare my lunches sometimes a few days in advance. This way I can just grab my lunch in the morning and easily stick to my diet throughout the day. If I forget to do this, I do get my lunch on the run as long as it fits in with the Clean and Green list of foods that you'll find at the beginning of the book.

Since I usually haven't got the time to make a big breakfast, I like to concentrate most of my carbs during lunch so that I have time to work them off during the rest of the day. Likewise, I've designed this menu so that you have the majority of your carbs at lunch rather than dinner times. A good rule of thumb for lunchtime is to fill up on a natural source of proteins, good fats, and natural carbohydrates. If you do that, your body will burn off the energy steadily and you will stay full until dinner. Be sure to keep track of your Slimbites!

Butternut Squash, Smoked Paprika and Chilli Soup

Serves: **2**

 Slimbites: **5**

1 butternut squash, peeled and seeded (400g)
1/2 tsp. chilli oil
2 tbsp. olive oil
1/2 tsp. ground chilli pepper
1/2 tsp. ground ginger
1/8 tsp. ground cinnamon

1 tsp. salt
1/3 nutmeg
160ml coconut milk
1 tbsp. smoked paprika
pumpkin seeds, to serve

♥ Preheat oven to 200°C/fan 180°C/gas 6.
♥ Cut the butternut squash into medium-sized cubes and place them onto a baking tray.
♥ Mix olive oil and chilli oil, ginger, cinnamon, salt and nutmeg. Pour this over the chunks of butternut squash.
♥ Bake the squash for about 30 to 40 minutes or until softened.
♥ Blend squash pieces with coconut milk until smooth.
♥ To serve sprinkle some pumpkin seeds and paprika over the soup.

Top Tip: This nutria-bullet of a soup saves so much time in the kitchen. Butternut squash is a fantastic source of dietary fibre and contains lots of B6—perfect for bones, the nervous system and the immune system.

Caramelised Onion Potato Rosti

Serves: **6**

♥ Slimbites: **2.5**

1 medium onion
2 large waxy potatoes
3 tbsp. olive oil
1 tbsp. Dijon mustard
1 tbsp. cider vinegar
salt, to taste

♥ Cut the onion into half-rings and place into a pan with the olive oil. When the onion becomes translucent, lower the heat and add the Dijon mustard, vinegar and salt and let everything slowly caramelise. When the onion gets stuck to the bottom of the pan, add a bit of water. Onion caramelisation takes about 20 minutes.

♥ Meanwhile grate the peeled potatoes.

♥ Mix the caramelised onions with the potatoes and transfer the mixture into a clean pan with some preheated olive oil. Spread potatoes in an even layer.

♥ After a couple of minutes, shake the pan to loosen the rosti from sides and bottom. Use a spatula if you need to. After 5–7 minutes, flip the rosti using another plate.

♥ Fry the rosti for 7–10 more minutes and serve with greens, salad or poached eggs.

Top Tip: Don't be shy to cook white potato, especially in the winter. There are only 14g of carbs per slice — a whole 76g fewer than your recommended 100g of carbohydrate a day (if you want to lose weight, that is)!

Curried Parsnip Soup

Serves: **4**

 Slimbites: **3**

2 medium parsnips
1 medium onion
2 small carrots
3 garlic cloves, minced
1 small apple, cored
360ml water
240ml coconut milk

1 tbsp. olive oil
1 tsp. curry powder
1/2 tsp. ground ginger
1/2 tsp. coriander seeds
1/4 tsp. each of ground cinnamon, nutmeg,
cashews, coriander and chilli to serve

♥ Peel and wash vegetables. Roughly chop all the
  veggies and cored apple into same-sized pieces.
♥ Heat olive oil in a pot and sauté the onion
  until translucent. Add the minced garlic and
  all the spices. Stir until completely mixed in.
♥ Add chopped vegetables, stir and pour in
  the water.
♥ When vegetables become soft (after about
  25–30 minutes), pour in coconut milk and
  puree with a blender.
♥ Serve warm, topped with some chopped
  cashews, coriander and chillies (optional).

Top Tip: You can swap any of the soup recipes with vegetable
broth if you are not keen on coconut milk (I love coconut
milk!). This soup is definitely my favourite with the sweetness
of the parsnip making it delicious. Parsnip is full of anti-
inflammatory, anti-fungal and anti-cancer cell compounds.

Spicy Vegetable Ratatouille

Serves: **4**

 Slimbites: **4**

1 tbsp. olive oil
1 white onion, thinly sliced
2 cloves garlic, crushed
1 red chilli
1 tsp. chilli powder
2 large courgettes, sliced
1 aubergine, sliced

1/2 red pepper
1/2 green pepper
1/2 yellow pepper
1 can chopped tomatoes (400g)
salt and pepper, to taste
chopped basil, to serve

- ♥ Heat a tablespoon of oil in a large pan.
- ♥ Cook the onions over a medium heat for 3–4 minutes until softened.
- ♥ Add the garlic, chilli and chilli powder and cook for another 1–2 minutes.
- ♥ Add the courgettes, aubergines and peppers, cook stirring frequently for 3–4 minutes.
- ♥ Add the chopped tomatoes and salt and pepper.
- ♥ Simmer on a low heat for 15 minutes.
- ♥ Serve topped with chopped basil.

Vegetable-Stuffed Sweet Potatoes

Serves: **4**

 Slimbites: **4**

4 large sweet potatoes
1 tbsp. olive oil
1/2 carrot, finely diced
1/2 red bell pepper, finely diced
1/2 yellow bell pepper, finely diced

1/2 green bell pepper, finely diced
2 spring onions, finely chopped
1 mild chilli, finely chopped
1 tsp. smoked paprika
1 tsp. cumin

- ♥ Preheat the oven to 170°C/fan 150°C/gas 4.
- ♥ Prick the potatoes all over with a fork and place in the oven for approximately 1 hour or until soft.
- ♥ In the meantime, heat a tablespoon of olive oil in a large pan and cook the carrot over a medium heat for 3–4 minutes.
- ♥ Add the peppers, spring onion and chillis and cook for a further 3–4 minutes.
- ♥ Mix in the smoked paprika and cumin.
- ♥ Slice the sweet potatoes in the middle and squeeze them so some potato comes out of the skin.
- ♥ Top with the vegetable mixture.

Cashew Crusted Chicken Caesar Salad

Serves: **1**

 Slimbites: **8**

1 (120g) chicken fillet
1 egg
1 handful of cashew nuts (around 18 kernels)
1/2 tsp. sea salt
1/2 tsp. dried basil
1/2 tsp. dried oregano

1/2 tsp. dried thyme
1/4 tsp. dried rosemary
1/4 tsp. dried tarragon
1/2 head of a romaine lettuce
6 cherry tomatoes

♥ Preheat oven to 200°C/fan 180°C/gas 4.
♥ Chop up the cashew nuts using a blender. Mix chopped nuts with salt and dried herbs.
♥ Beat one egg and dip chicken fillet into it. Let the excess egg drip off and coat chicken with chopped nuts.
♥ Place cashew-coated chicken into a pan covered with foil. Bake for 20–25 minutes.

♥ After baking leave to cool a little and then slice.
♥ Place torn lettuce and chicken slices in a bowl and top with cherry tomatoes.

Top Tip: Don't be frightened of the high Slimbites — these are a fantastic source of heart-protecting monounsaturated fats. Eating cashews can reduce high triglyceride levels. Your triglycerides are a type of fat found in your blood. Eating a high-fat carb diet can lead to high triglyceride levels and quick weight gain.

Caesar Salad Dressing

Serves: **1**

♥ Slimbites: **2**

1 egg yolk
1 tsp. lemon juice
1/4 tsp. anchovy paste
1 tbsp. olive oil
1 garlic clove, finely minced
1 tsp. Dijon mustard
pinch of salt and black pepper

♥ In a food processor, combine the egg yolk, lemon juice, anchovy paste, Dijon mustard, minced garlic and salt and pepper.

♥ Blend until smooth, add olive oil and blend again to combine. Drizzle on top of the salad and toss!

Chicken Avocado Burgers

Serves: **4**

 Slimbites: **4**

450g minced chicken breast
1/4 small red onion, diced
1/4 medium red bell pepper, diced
1/4 medium green bell pepper, diced
1 egg

salt and pepper, to taste
1 large tomato, thickly sliced
1 avocado, sliced
juice of a lime

♥ In a large mixing bowl combine the ground chicken breast, red onion, red bell pepper, green bell pepper, egg, salt and pepper. Using your hands is the best way to mix; don't be afraid to get dirty!
♥ Form the chicken mixture into four equal-sized patties.
♥ Switch the grill on (I have a George Foreman grill which I like to use for this recipe) and place the burgers on the grill. Cook for 10 minutes on each side, until the burgers reach an internal temperature of 74°C and look cooked the whole way through.

♥ While the burgers are cooking, slice up the tomato and avocados. Drizzle the lime juice over the avocado slices to prevent browning.
♥ Once the burgers are cooked, place one on each plate. Stack a tomato slice on top of each burger patty.
♥ Next, stack avocado slices on top of the tomato and serve.

Grilled Chicken Skewers

Serves: **4**

 Slimbites: **4**

2 rosemary sprigs
2 small garlic cloves
pinch of salt
450g chicken fillets
1 medium green pepper
1 medium red onion

1 small courgette
8 cherry tomatoes
1/2 lemon
2 tbsp. olive oil
salt and pepper, to taste

♥ Soak the skewers in cold water.
♥ Put the rosemary sprigs, salt, pepper and
  garlic cloves in a mortar and crush with a
  pestle. Mix the rosemary puree with olive
  oil and lemon juice.
♥ Cut chicken fillets into 2.5cm cubes and place
  them in the marinade for at least 30 minutes or
  up to 3 hours.
♥ Cut the veggies, except the tomatoes, into bite-
  sized pieces.
♥ String the chicken onto skewers, alternating
  with vegetable pieces.
♥ Place the skewers on a hot grill and cook for
  9–12 minutes, turning every 3–4 minutes.

Courgette Pad Thai

Serves: **1**

 Slimbites: **6**

1 medium courgette
1 egg
1 red fire chilli
1 garlic clove
1/2 red onion
120g prawns, washed and peeled
2 tbsp. olive oil or sesame oil
2 tbsp. peanuts (chopped)

2 tbsp. fish sauce
2 tbsp. water
1 tbsp. lime juice
1 tsp. ginger (grated)
1 tbsp. each of Tamari, spring onions,
    coriander, lime wedges for serving.

♥ Cut the courgette into noodles with a
  spiralizer, mandolin or knife.
♥ Get a wok nice and hot and add the oil, garlic
  chilli and prawns.
♥ Add the onion until soft. Then add the ginger.
♥ When prawns turn pink, pour fish sauce
  mixture and stir on a medium heat for a
  couple of minutes.
♥ Push the prawns and onions to one side of the
  pan and add the courgette noodles and water.
♥ Mix and stir fry all the pan mix, then add the
  egg in the middle and stir in. Add the Tamari.
♥ Squeeze in the lime juice.
♥ Sprinkle chopped nuts, spring onions and
  coriander over the top with a lime wedge
  to serve.

Avocado and Prawn Boats

Serves: **4**

 Slimbites: **5**

2 avocados
80g boiled prawns (peeled)
1 small chopped red onion
1 small chopped pepper
1 small chopped tomato

1 small garlic clove, minced
1 tsp. chopped parsley
2 pineapple rings
2 tbsp. lemon juice
1 tbsp. olive oil

- ♥ Slice avocados in half and pit them. Place the pitted avocados under a hot grill for a couple of minutes.
- ♥ Meanwhile mix chopped vegetables with minced garlic, pineapple, parsley, olive oil, lemon juice, and salt and pepper to taste. Then mix in the boiled prawns.
- ♥ Place a couple of spoonfuls of the salsa into avocado halves and serve.

Top Tip: This is the perfect lunchtime snack — it's so quick and easy to prepare. The avocado offers nearly 20 different vitamins and minerals with each serving. Your hair, skin and nails will look healthier and healthier with each serving. Whenever my skin is in need of some TLC I always fill up on the good fats of an avocado!

Pork and Prawn Spring Rolls

Serves: **Makes 8 rolls**

 Slimbites: **1.5**

1 head Napa/Chinese cabbage
300g prawns, peeled
1/2 tsp. sesame oil
1 tbsp. coconut oil
500g minced lean pork
2–3 garlic cloves, minced
red pepper, to taste
1 tsp. ginger, grated

2 tbsp. Tamari
1/2 tsp. fish sauce
60ml dashi stock (traditional Japanese stock;
   I use the pre-made stocks to save time –
   vegetable stock can also be used)
4 spring onions (white parts), chopped

♥ Separate 6–8 large cabbage leaves and pop them to one side. Shred 3–4 small leaves of the Chinese cabbage.
♥ Chop the peeled prawns and fry them with the pork in a preheated pan of coconut and sesame oil. After a minute, add the minced garlic, red pepper, grated ginger, Tamari, fish sauce, and dashi stock. Add the shredded cabbage and wait for half of the liquid to evaporate and the pork to cook through.
♥ Mix your pork filling with chopped spring onion and set aside.
♥ Steam the cabbage leaves for about 1 minute: they should be soft but not mushy. Trim off any excess hard stem. I use a tiered pan steamer.

♥ Place a good spoonful of pork on the stem-end and then roll it, folding the excess green leafy parts from the sides over the filling. You may need a couple of attempts but you will soon find a good rhythm when folding. If I am throwing a party I like to pop a cocktail stick through to secure a perfect parcel!
♥ You can serve the rolls immediately or re-steam them later.

Top Tip: This is not only a light lunch but a perfect party snack. Chinese cabbage or Napa cabbage is perfect for bone development, making your bones stronger and healthier. Chinese cabbage also contains natural electrolytes.

Chorizo and Sweet Potato Frittata

Serves: **6**

 Slimbites: **4**

60g chorizo, sliced (make sure the chorizo
doesn't contain preservatives or dextrose)
6 large eggs
1/2 medium pepper
1/2 small red onion

1/2 sweet potato, chopped into small pieces
6 broccoli florets
60ml coconut milk
handful of spinach
salt and pepper, to taste

♥ Preheat oven to 170°C/fan 150°C/gas 4.
♥ Fry the chorizo slices in a heated pan until
golden brown and then place them on a paper
towel to absorb excess grease.
♥ Use half of the leftover fat in a pan to fry
chopped pepper, onion and sweet potato.
♥ After 8 minutes add spinach leaves and
continue cooking until they wilt.
♥ Boil the broccoli florets and add them to the
vegetables with chorizo slices.
♥ Beat the eggs with some salt, pepper and
coconut milk.
♥ Pour the beaten eggs on top of vegetable mix
and place the whole pan in the preheated
oven for around 15 minutes or until egg is set
in the middle.

Sausage and Mash

Serves: **1**

♥ Slimbites: **15**

2 lean pork sausages (100g)
1 tsp. olive oil

For potato mash:
2 medium potatoes
80ml vegetable broth
1 tsp. olive oil

♥ Peel and chop the potatoes and then cook them in salted boiling water until softened (10–12 minutes). Drain and puree the softened potatoes with 1 teaspoon of olive oil and vegetable broth.

♥ Pour a teaspoon of olive oil into a separate pan and fry the sausages over a low heat for about 15 minutes until golden brown (or a bit longer if you like them well-done like me!).

♥ To serve, place the potato mash in a bowl and top with the sausages. You can add the onion gravy too...

Top Tip: I love this good old British dish more than anything, although I find it too heavy for an evening meal. I try and keep my dinners low in carbs so usually make this for myself for lunch.

Gravy

Serves: **1**

 Slimbites: **3**

1 tbsp. olive oil
1/2 small onion
240ml beef stock
1 tbsp. potato flour

1/4 tsp. chopped garlic
sea salt and black pepper, to taste
fresh thyme and rosemary

♥ Heat the oil in a medium pan over a medium heat and sauté onions and garlic for 10 minutes or until golden brown.
♥ Add in the stock and potato flour and simmer for 10 minutes over low heat. When the volume comes down to almost half add in thyme, rosemary and season to taste. Stir to combine.

Prawn Thai Soup

Serves: **3**

 Slimbites: **3**

1/2 medium red onion
1 tsp. coconut oil
1/2 tsp. grated ginger
1/2 tsp. fish sauce
3 small garlic cloves
1/2 tsp. cumin
1 tsp. curry powder
1 tsp. basil

480ml coconut milk
240ml vegetable broth
300g prawns
9–10 medium mussels
1 small pepper
1 small chilli pepper
chopped coriander for serving

♥ Chop the onion and pepper into small cubes and fry in coconut oil until onions become translucent.
♥ Make a paste out of the ginger, fish sauce, garlic and spices using a mortar or a powerful blender. Add the aromatic paste to the onions and after 30 seconds cover everything with a mixture of coconut milk and vegetable broth.
♥ Let the soup base simmer for a couple of minutes, while you are peeling the prawns.
♥ Add the prawns and mussels, cover and cook for 5 minutes or more.
♥ Serve with extra hot pepper and chopped coriander.

Salt Fish Fritters

Serves: **2**

 Slimbites: **6**

170g boneless and skinless salted white fish
(cod, sea bass, etc.), soaked overnight in
fresh water
100g almond flour
1 tbsp. potato flour
60ml water
1/3 tsp. baking soda

1 tsp. lemon juice
1 tsp. smoked paprika
1/2 small red onion, chopped
1 small chilli pepper, chopped
zest of 1/2 lemon
olive oil, for frying
salt and pepper, for seasoning

♥ Drain off the salt fish. Cook the fish in a pan
of boiling water for 15–20 minutes. Take off
the boil and drain once more.
♥ Chill the fish and flake into pieces with a fork
when ready.
♥ Mix the almond flour, potato flour, baking
soda, chopped chillies, and smoked paprika.
Pour in the water and 1/2 zest of lemon juice,
stirring until a smooth and thick paste forms.
♥ Add the chopped chilli, onions and fish to the
batter mix while stirring.

♥ Heat about 3cm of olive oil in a pan and place
large spoonfuls of fish batter into it to form
fritters. Fry until fritters get crispy and golden-
brown. Place them onto paper towels to soak
off excess oil.
♥ To serve, sprinkle with freshly ground
black pepper and maybe add your favourite
Clean and Green sauce!

*Top Tip: Salt fish is brilliant because you can keep it in the
cupboards for ages. It's a Clean and Green food that really
does have a long shelf life.*

Hot Beef and Vegetable Chilli

Serves: **4–5**

 Slimbites: **6**

2 tbsp. coconut oil
1 large white onion, finely chopped
1 tsp. chilli powder
1 tsp. dried crushed chipotle chillis
1 tsp. cumin
1 tsp. sea salt
400g beef stewing steak, cut into rough chunks
2 cloves garlic, crushed
2 cans chopped tomatoes
200ml vegetable stock
1 tsp. oregano

2 red chillies, finely chopped
50g green jalapeños
4–5 medium mushrooms, sliced
1 large carrot, peeled and sliced
1 small yellow courgette, sliced
1 small green courgette, sliced
1 red pepper, diced
3 large kale leaves
fresh coriander
spring onions, roughly chopped

♥ Heat the 2 tablespoons of coconut oil in a large heavy-bottomed pan.
♥ Cook the finely chopped onions over a medium heat until softened.
♥ While the onions are softening, combine the chilli powder, chipotle, cumin and salt in a bowl and roll the meat into the combined flavours.
♥ When the onions are soft, add the garlic and cook for around 2–3 minutes.

♥ Add the tomatoes, vegetable stock, oregano, chillies, jalapeños, mushrooms and sliced carrots.
♥ Turn the heat down to low and cook, stirring occasionally, for 30–40 minutes.
♥ Add the courgettes and pepper, cook for a further 10 minutes. Add more stock if required.
♥ Finally add the kale and cook for 5 minutes.
♥ Garnish with chopped spring onions and coriander leaves.

Top Tip: Save time and effort by cooking enough to last you or you and your family for a few days. I often freeze a few portions to have at a later date and to also take into work for lunch.

Burgers with Pineapple Salsa

Serves: **4**

 Slimbites: **6**

 Slimbites: **1**

For burgers:
450g lean beef, minced
1/2 tsp. salt
1/2 tsp. black pepper
1 egg
2 tbsp. ground almonds
1 tbsp. olive oil

For salsa:
1 small can pineapple rings, drained
1/2 red pepper
1 Granny Smith apple
1 small handful of coriander
juice of half a lime

- ♥ Place all the ingredients for the burgers except the oil into a large bowl.
- ♥ Mix the ingredients for the burgers together using your hands until fully combined.
- ♥ Divide the mixture into four balls and flatten to form your burger patties.
- ♥ Place on a plate and cover with cling film.
- ♥ Refrigerate for at least 1 hour.
- ♥ Place the burger patties onto a grill. I have a George Foreman grill that I love to use for this recipe and I simply close the lid on the grill and cook for around 7–10 minutes, checking frequently.
- ♥ No need to flip as the grill cooks from both sides.

- ♥ Dice the pineapple, pepper and apple into small pieces and chop the coriander.
- ♥ Combine the ingredients in a small bowl and drizzle with lime juice.
- ♥ Place the burgers on a serving plate (or in paleo buns if you want) and top with salsa.

Top Tip: Please make sure the pineapple rings are not preserved in syrup. Always read your food labels for those sneaky sugars!

Wheat-Free Paleo Bread

Serves: **13**

 Slimbites: **2**

3 tbsp. pumpkin seed flour
1 tbsp. potato flour
40g ground flaxseeds
1 and 1/2 tsp. chia seeds
1 tsp. baking soda

2 tsp. dried mixed herbs, crushed
salt, to taste
7 eggs
2 tbsp. balsamic vinegar
1 tbsp. coconut oil, melted

♥ Preheat the oven to 170°C/fan 150°C/gas 4.
♥ Line a loaf pan with lightly greased parchment paper.
♥ In a bowl, mix together the flours, seeds, baking soda and salt.
♥ In another bowl, add remaining ingredients and beat till well combined.

♥ Add egg mixture into the bowl with flour mixture till well combined.
♥ Transfer the mixture into prepared loaf pan evenly.
♥ Bake for about 45 minutes or till a toothpick inserted in the centre comes out clean.

Lamb Curry Meatballs

Serves: **6**

 Slimbites: **10**

For meatballs:
450g minced lamb
1 egg
2 tsp. paprika
1 tsp. ground ginger
1 tsp. turmeric
1 tsp. cumin
1 tsp. cayenne pepper
pinch of ground nutmeg
1/2 tsp. salt

For curry:
1 tbsp. coconut oil
1 onion, diced
2 garlic cloves, minced
1 tsp. fresh ginger, minced
4 tsp. curry powder
2 tsp. turmeric
1 tbsp. chicken stock
1 can coconut milk
sea salt, to taste
black pepper, to taste

♥ In a large mixing bowl combine the minced lamb, egg, paprika, ground ginger, turmeric, cumin, cayenne pepper, ground nutmeg and 1/2 teaspoon salt.
♥ Use your hands to mix the ingredients, until everything is well combined.
♥ Using your hands, form the mixture into 12 small meatballs and set aside.
♥ Heat the coconut oil in a frying pan over a medium heat.
♥ Add the meatballs and cook for about 3–5 minutes per side.
♥ Once the meatballs are browned, remove and set aside.
♥ Add the onions to the frying pan. Sauté until they begin to turn translucent, about 8–10 minutes.
♥ Stir in the garlic, minced ginger, curry powder and turmeric.
♥ Sautee for 1–2 minutes, until the spices become fragrant.

♥ Add the chicken stock or water. Use a wooden spoon to deglaze the pan and scrape up all the brown bits.
♥ Pour in the coconut milk and season with salt and pepper.
♥ Add the meatballs back to the pot and simmer everything for an additional 10 minutes.
♥ Serve the meatball curry on its own or with a side of cauliflower rice.

Lamb and Apricot Vegetable Quinoa

Serves: **4**

 Slimbites: **6**

340g lean lamb
115g uncooked quinoa
360ml water or broth
1 tsp. chilli oil
2 tbsp. olive oil
5 dried apricots, diced
1 medium onion

1 small carrot, grated
1/2 large pepper
3 small cloves garlic, minced
1/2 cinnamon stick
1 star anise
2 cloves
coriander leaves, to serve

- ♥ Heat the olive oil and chilli oil in a pan over a medium heat. Chop the onion and pepper, and fry them in the oil until onion is translucent.
- ♥ Add the grated carrot, minced garlic, diced apricots, cinnamon, anise and cloves to the pan.
- ♥ Cut the lean lamb into squares and brown with spiced vegetables. Add quinoa and pour in the water or vegetable broth, stirring until mixed in.
- ♥ Let the quinoa boil in the pan for 25–30 minutes, until all the liquid is absorbed. Serve with chopped coriander leaves as a garnish.

Top Tip: Quinoa is actually a seed but people are always confusing quinoa with a grain. It is a gluten-free super seed and high in protein so a perfect rice or pasta substitute.

Hawaiian Pizza (no wheat or dairy!)

Serves: **4**

 Slimbites: **4**

For crust:
185g chickpea (or any pea) flour
240ml coconut milk
2 tsp. baking powder
salt, to taste

For topping:
ham
vegan cheese
pineapple, chopped
5 tsp. tomato sauce
1 medium pepper

♥ Preheat oven to 170°C/fan 150°C/gas 4.
♥ Combine dry ingredients: chickpea flour,
  salt and baking powder. Pour some warm
  coconut milk into the dry ingredients and
  mix everything up until you get a thick
  and smooth dough.
♥ Spoon the dough onto a greased pizza pan and
  smooth it out with the back of a spoon.
♥ Place crust into the oven and bake for
  15–18 minutes.
♥ Cover the pizza base with tomato sauce
  and scatter all the toppings on top. Bake for
  another 5 minutes, until the cheese melts.

Chickpea flour is a great substitute for normal
everyday grain flour. I find I don't get the same
bloating as when I use full or dietary fibre. On top
of that, chickpea flour also improves heart health
and stabilises your blood sugars.

Celeriac Soup with Cauliflower, Nuts and Prosciutto

Serves: **2**

 Slimbites: **5**

75g chopped celeriac
300g cauliflower florets
1/2 medium onion, chopped
120ml coconut cream or milk
240ml chicken or vegetable broth
small handful hazelnuts

1/4 tsp. nutmeg (freshly ground)
2 tbsp. olive oil
2 slices of prosciutto
2 thyme sprigs
2 small garlic cloves, minced

♥ In a large pan, heat half of the olive oil and add the chopped onion. Sauté onions until translucent.

♥ Add the minced garlic and thyme leaves. After 30 seconds, mix in the celeriac and cauliflower florets.

♥ Pour in the broth and canned coconut milk/cream. Season and simmer over a low heat for 20–25 minutes or until the vegetables are softened.

♥ Take the pan from the heat and blitz vegetables with a blender.

♥ Use the other half of the olive oil in a pan to fry prosciutto until golden-brown and crispy. Place prosciutto pieces on paper towels and crumble.

♥ Mix the hazelnuts with the olive oil and the prosciutto grease left on the pan. When hazelnuts become slightly golden, remove from heat and chop.

♥ Spoon the soup into bowls, drizzle with some olive oil and top with crispy prosciutto and chopped hazelnuts.

Top Tip: Celeriac is so underrated and is absolutely delicious. It is hard to believe it's a member of the celery family! The vegetable is full of antioxidants and iron, and research shows it contains anti-cancer agents. It is definitely my favourite root vegetable.

Dinner

You may have learned by now that eating Clean and Green doesn't need to be difficult. There are so many easy, delicious, and stunning recipes out there that giving up processed foods barely seems like a sacrifice. I've included 21 of my favourite, completely clean dinner recipes in this chapter. Since dinner is near the end of the day, I have kept the recipes in this chapter quite low in carbohydrates. Remember, for the ultimate weight loss you want to stay under 100 grams of carbs per day. Check out the guide below to learn about the carbohydrate content in different vegetables. Where you see a '*' then this item is a 'free food', which means it is so low that you don't even have to count it in your daily meal plan and you can have as much of it as you want! Bon appetit!

Carbs per 100g:

Watercress*	1.3g	Peppers*	7g
Lettuce*	2.9g	Spring onion*	7g
Spinach*	3.6g	Kale*	8.75g
Celery*	3g	Brussels sprouts*	9g
Courgette*	3.1g	Swede*	9g
Radish*	3.4g	Onion*	9g
Cucumber*	3.6g	Celeriac*	9.2g
Tomatoes*	3.9g	Beetroot*	9.6g
Asparagus*	3.9g	Carrots	10g
Bean sprouts*		Artichoke*	11g
Cauliflower*	5g	Leek	14g
Aubergine*	6g	Peas*	14g
Cabbage*	6g	Parsnip	18g
Olives*	6g	White potato	17g
Mushrooms*	7g	Sweet potato	20g (I prefer sweet potato, it contains more fibre)
Broccoli*	7g		
Fennel*	7g		
Pumpkin	7g	Sweetcorn	19g
French beans*	7g	Yam	27.7g
Okra*	7g		

Butternut Squash Chilli

Serves: **4**

 Slimbites: **5**

2 tbsp. coconut oil or olive oil
2 large butternut squash (peeled and cut into
  2.5cm pieces)
1 large onion, diced
2 cloves of garlic
1 small dried chipotle chilli, diced

1 tbsp. chilli powder
2 medium peppers, diced
1 can chopped tomatoes
120ml vegetable stock
salt and pepper, to taste
coriander for garnish

♥ Preheat the oven to 190°C/fan 170°C/gas 5.
♥ Peel and chop the butternut squash into
  2.5cm cubes.
♥ Place the squash into a large roasting tray
  and coat with a tablespoon of oil.
♥ Cook for 25–35 minutes until browned and
  soft.
♥ In the meantime, chop the onion finely and
  crush the garlic.
♥ Heat a tablespoon of olive oil or coconut oil
  in a large pan and cook the onion and garlic
  over a medium heat until soft (approximately
  4–5 minutes).
♥ Chop the peppers and the dried chipotle chilli
  and add to the pan.

♥ Add the chilli powder and cook for another
  3–4 minutes.
♥ Pour in the tomatoes and vegetable stock.
  Cook for 15 minutes.
♥ Add the butternut squash. Heat through.
♥ Season with salt and pepper and serve with
  coriander on top.

Cauliflower Fried Rice

Serves: **2**

 Slimbites: **5.5**

1 large cauliflower head
1 tbsp. sesame oil
1 large carrot, cubed into 1cm pieces
2 tbsp. sweetcorn
1 large egg, beaten

2 tbsp. Tamari
1 tsp. chilli flakes
1 spring onion, finely chopped
coriander, finely chopped for garnish

♥ Cut the cauliflower into florets.
♥ Place cauliflower into a food processor and
  pulse until you have small rice-like pieces.
  You may need to do this in two batches.
  Take care not to over-process!
♥ In a large pan, heat the sesame oil over a
  medium heat. Cook the carrot, stirring
  frequently, for 3–4 minutes.
♥ Add the sweetcorn to the pan.
♥ Add the cauliflower and cook for 8–10
  minutes, making sure the cauliflower doesn't
  stick to the pan.

♥ Make a hole in the middle of the cauliflower
  and pour the egg into the hole. Leave for 30
  seconds and then scramble. Once cooked, mix
  the cauliflower thoroughly to distribute the egg.
♥ Stir in the Tamari and chilli flakes, as well as
  salt and pepper to taste.
♥ Garnish with spring onion and coriander.

Courgette Vegetable Lasagne

Serves: **6**

 Slimbites: **3**

2 large courgettes
70g cashew nuts, soaked in water for 24 hours
120ml almond milk
1/2 tsp. garlic powder
1 tbsp. olive oil
1 large onion, finely chopped

1 carrot, finely diced
2 cloves garlic, crushed
2 peppers, diced
1/2 aubergine, finely diced
1 can chopped tomatoes
salt and pepper, to taste

♥ Preheat oven to 175°C/fan 155°C/gas 4.
♥ Slice the courgette into 5mm-thick pieces using a mandolin food slicer.
♥ Salt both sides of the courgettes and lay them out on a large baking tray, taking care not to layer them.
♥ Leave the courgettes out for 20 minutes. Courgettes contain a lot of water and this process removes moisture before cooking.
♥ In the meantime, place the cashews in a heavy-duty food processor with the almond milk, salt, pepper and garlic powder, and process until smooth. Set aside.
♥ Heat the olive oil in a large pan over a medium heat and add the onions and carrots, cooking for 3–4 minutes until softened.
♥ Add the crushed garlic cloves and cook for a further 1–2 minutes.
♥ Add the peppers and aubergine and cook for 3–4 minutes.
♥ Pour in the tomatoes and mix in salt and pepper.

♥ Leave to simmer for 15 minutes.
♥ Gently run two fingers down either side of the dried courgette slices to remove excess water and lay pieces on a paper towel.
♥ Return the courgettes to the baking tray. Add salt and place in the oven for 5 minutes to dry out further.
♥ In a 24cm square glass ovenproof dish, add a few tablespoons of the vegetable sauce, followed by a single layer of the courgette. Cover the courgette layer with sauce and top with another courgette layer. Repeat until all the sauce is used. Finish with a final layer of courgette.
♥ Top the lasagne with the cashew mixture, ensuring that the top layer of courgettes is covered.
♥ Cook for 30–40 minutes until the top has browned slightly.
♥ Garnish with basil and serve.

Sunday Special Roast Chicken with Cauliflower Rice

Serves: **4**

 Slimbites: **10**

For the cauliflower rice:
2 tbsp. olive oil
1 medium carrot, grated
1 medium onion, chopped
1 tsp. grated ginger
2 small garlic cloves, minced
1 tsp. curry powder
1/2 tsp. ground coriander seeds
1/4 tsp. ground fenugreek
4 tbsp. sultanas or dried cranberries
1 small head cauliflower
chopped coriander and lemon juice to taste

For the chicken:
1 whole chicken (about 3 lbs. or 1.3kg)
2 tsp. salt
1 tsp. garlic powder
1 tsp. cayenne
2 tbsp. olive oil

♥ Preheat your oven to 200°C/fan 180°C/gas 6.
♥ Cut the cauliflower into florets and pop them into a food processor. Turn on the power a few seconds at a time until the cauliflower takes a rice-shape form.
♥ Heat the olive oil in a pan and add the grated carrot and the onion.
♥ After 2 minutes add the grated ginger and minced garlic. Wait 30 seconds more and then mix in the curry powder, coriander, fenugreek, sultanas and blended cauliflower florets. Remove from the heat and add salt to taste.
♥ Place the cauliflower filling into chicken cavity and tie legs together using string.

♥ Roast for 15 minutes, then lower the temperature to 180°C/fan 160°C/gas 5 and continue cooking for about 40–45 minutes, until the juices from chicken run clear.
♥ Remove filling from the cavity, mix with chopped coriander and lemon juice and serve with the chicken.

Roasted Vegetables with Vegetarian Gravy

Serves: **2**

 Slimbites: **4**

2 medium potatoes
1 medium beetroot
1 medium onion
1 medium red pepper
1/2 medium celeriac
3 small carrots
3 small garlic cloves

2 bay leaves
2 tbsp. olive oil
1 tsp. rosemary leaves
1 tsp. cider vinegar
1 tsp. potato flour
160ml vegetable stock
salt and pepper, to taste

♥ Preheat your oven to 180°C/fan 160°C/gas 6. Roughly chop the peeled vegetables and mix them with olive oil, salt and pepper. Add the whole garlic cloves (with skin on), bay leaves and rosemary, then transfer onto a baking sheet.
♥ Bake veggies for about 35–45 minutes, until softened. I recommend baking the beets separately otherwise it can turn all the other ingredients and the gravy purple.
♥ When vegetables are cooked, put them on a serving platter, remove the onions, garlic and bay.

♥ Place the baking sheet over a low heat on a stove.
♥ Add the baked onion and roasted garlic into a pan and pour on the vegetable stock. Stir in the potato flour to thicken.
♥ Stir to release all the caramelised bits from the bottom, add vinegar and wait until gravy becomes thick and bubbly. Strain the gravy before serving.

Blackened Chicken with Mango Salsa

Serves: **2**

♥ Slimbites: **5**

2 chicken breasts
1 tsp. smoked paprika
1/2 tsp. salt
1/2 tsp. cumin
1/2 tsp. thyme
1/2 tsp. onion powder
1/2 tsp. cayenne pepper

1/4 tsp. black pepper
2 tsp. coconut oil
1 medium mango, peeled, stoned, and cubed
1 jalapeño pepper, diced
1/4 red onion, diced
2 tsp. coriander, chopped
1 lime, juiced

♥ Preheat oven to 180°C/fan 160°C/gas 4.
♥ Combine the smoked paprika, salt, cumin, thyme, onion powder, cayenne pepper and black pepper together in a small bowl.
♥ Trim the extra fat off the chicken breasts. Place the trimmed chicken breasts on a plate or cutting board. Sprinkle the seasoning mixture over the chicken breasts, patting the spices onto the chicken as you go and flip them over completely covering both sides.
♥ Heat the coconut oil in an ovenproof frying pan over a medium-high heat. Place the chicken breasts in the pan and sear for about 3 minutes. Flip the chicken and sear the other side for an additional 3 minutes.

♥ Transfer the entire pan into the oven and bake for 10–15 minutes.
♥ While the chicken is cooking, in a small bowl stir to combine the mango, jalapeño, red onion, coriander and lime juice.
♥ Once the chicken is cooked, remove from the oven and place on separate plates. Top with the mango salsa and serve.

Chicken Caprese

Serves: **4**

 Slimbites: **5.5**

4 boneless skinless chicken breasts
2 and 1/2 tbsp. of olive oil
2 and 1/2 tbsp. of cider vinegar
3 tbsp. Dijon mustard
2 garlic cloves, minced

4 fresh basil leaves, chopped
400g tomatoes, chopped
1 tsp. sea salt
fresh cracked black pepper, to taste

- In a small bowl, mix together the vinegar, olive oil, half the basil leaves, half the minced garlic and the Dijon mustard.
- Add the chicken to a small bowl or zip-lock bag. Pour the cider vinegar mixture over the chicken. Turn to coat the chicken with the marinade. Cover the bowl or close the zip-lock bag.
- Place the chicken into the refrigerator to marinate for at least 2 hours.
- Preheat the oven to 190°C/fan 160°C/gas 5.
- In a small bowl, stir to combine the tomatoes with the remaining basil, garlic, and salt.

- Place the marinated chicken in a shallow baking dish or sheet. Evenly pile the tomato mixture on top of each chicken breast.
- Bake uncovered in the oven for 25–30 minutes, or until the chicken juices run clear.
- Garnish with fresh cracked black pepper.

Chicken Spaghetti Pumpkin Florentine

Serves: **2**

 Slimbites: **6**

1 small pumpkin
1/2 medium onion, diced
1 tbsp. coconut oil
120g baby spinach

1 chicken breast
1/2 lemon, juice only
salt and pepper to taste
fresh basil, for garnish

♥ Preheat the oven to 200°C/fan 180°C/gas 6.
♥ Cut the pumpkin in half, lengthwise. Place it face down on a baking tray lined with parchment paper. Bake in the oven for 45–60 minutes, until the pumpkin is tender.
♥ Meanwhile, heat the coconut oil in a sauté pan over a medium heat. Add the chicken and cook through until white. Remove the pan from the heat and place the chicken on a chopping board. Use two forks to shred the chicken.
♥ Place the pan back on the heat and add the shredded chicken. Then add the onion and cook until translucent.
♥ Add the chicken and spinach and continue cooking until the spinach is wilted. Season with salt and pepper to taste.
♥ Once the pumpkin is cooked, flip it over, scoop out the seeds and discard.

♥ Use a fork to loosen and scrape the insides of the pumpkin halves to create spaghetti-like shapes. Spoon half of the chicken mixture into each of the pumpkin pieces, mixing with the pumpkin spaghetti. Garnish with fresh basil and serve.

Portabello Burgers

Serves: **2**

 Slimbites: **8**

For the burgers:
300g minced lean beef
1 tsp. onion powder
1 tsp. garlic powder

For the portabello mushrooms:
4 large portabello mushrooms
1 tbsp. coconut oil
1 tsp. cider vinegar
salt and pepper, to taste

For the caramelised onions:
1 large onion, sliced into slivers
2 tbsp. coconut oil
1 tsp. garlic powder
1 tsp. salt
1 tbsp. cider vinegar
1 tsp. black pepper

For the burger:
♥ In a large bowl, mix the minced beef with the onion powder and garlic powder. Form burger patties using your hands to shape 2 medium sized burgers.
♥ Place on a preheated double grill, flipping when necessary.

For the mushroom:
♥ Preheat oven to 180°C/fan 160°C/gas 4.
♥ Remove the excess stem from the bottom of the mushroom until you have two mushroom buns for your burger.
♥ Prepare a baking tray with coconut oil. Place the mushrooms bottom side up on the baking tray and sprinkle cider vinegar, salt, and pepper over the top.
♥ Bake the mushrooms for 10–12 minutes.

For the onions :
♥ Meanwhile, heat a frying pan on a medium heat and add 2 tablespoons of coconut oil.
♥ Add the sliced onion, stir and cook for 1 minute.
♥ Season the onions with garlic powder, salt, cider vinegar and black pepper. Stir and continue cooking on medium heat. After 5 minutes, set the onions on a low heat and simmer while you prepare the rest of the burger.
♥ When cooked, place a burger between two mushrooms to create a mushroom burger.
♥ Sprinkle the caramelised onions on top of each burger and cover with another mushroom top.
♥ Serve and enjoy.

Scrumptious Sweet Potato Shepherd's Pie

Serves: **4**

 Slimbites: **8**

2 large sweet potatoes
2 tbsp. olive oil
1 onion, roughly chopped
2 medium carrots, chopped

450g lean minced beef
4 sprigs fresh thyme
fresh rosemary
rock salt and black pepper

♥ Preheat the oven to 170°C/fan 150°C/gas 4.
♥ Boil the sweet potato in a pan until soft or just tender. Drain and mash with 2 tablespoons of olive oil or you can use coconut oil. Add a little of the cooking stock from the pan if needed. Season with rock salt and pepper.
♥ Heat some oil in a pan and sauté the onions until soft.
♥ Add the minced meat and cook for another 5 minutes. Add the diced carrots and cook again for 5 minutes.
♥ Pour in some more of the stock from the sweet potatoes, about 120ml, and simmer uncovered for about 5 minutes.

♥ Spread the cooked meat in a dish and cover with the mashed sweet potato.
♥ Drizzle some more olive oil over the top and a sprinkle of rock salt, and bake in the oven for 30 minutes.
♥ Remove from the oven and garnish with paprika.

Melt in Your Mouth Meatloaf

Serves: **8**

 Slimbites: **7**

1 medium onion, finely diced
900g lean minced beef
1 cup almond meal
2 eggs
1 small can tomato puree

1 tbsp. mashed garlic or garlic paste
2 tbsp. fresh basil
1 tsp. dried oregano
olive oil for cooking
rock salt and black pepper for seasoning

- ♥ Preheat the oven to 220°C/fan 200°C/gas 7.
- ♥ In a bowl, mix all the ingredients together except the oil.
- ♥ Lightly grease a loaf-sized glass baking dish and place the mixture into it, patting it down gently so it reaches the corners.
- ♥ Sprinkle the top of the loaf with olive oil and bake in a hot oven for an hour until cooked through.
- ♥ Leave to cool for 10 minutes and then serve.

Grilled Flank Steak with Pineapple Salsa

Serves: **3**

♥ Slimbites: **6**

For the steak:
1 tbsp. olive oil
chipotle powder
450g beef flank steak
1/2 tsp. chilli powder
4 fresh pineapple rings

For the salsa:
200g finely chopped fresh pineapple
2 tbsp. red onion, finely chopped
2 tbsp. spring onion, finely chopped
1 tbsp. red pepper, finely chopped (optional)
1 tbsp. fresh coriander, finely chopped
a pinch of ground red pepper, cayenne or
    chilli powder
2 tbsp. finely minced jalapeño pepper (optional)
juice of 1 fresh lime
1/4 tsp. black pepper

♥ For the salsa, combine all ingredients and refrigerate for at least an hour.
♥ Turn the grill onto high.
♥ Mix the oil and chipotle powder together in a small dish.
♥ Brush onto both sides of the steak.
♥ Grill 3 minutes on one side, and 2 minutes on the other.
♥ Remove the steak and place on a plate. Cover and let rest for 10 minutes.
♥ Grill the pineapple rings for 45 seconds to 1 minute per side.

♥ Cut the pineapple into small chunks and place in a medium bowl.
♥ Slice the steak thinly, and serve with the pineapple salsa.

Bristol's Beef Stew

Serves: **4**

 Slimbites: **8.5**

1 tbsp. olive oil
1 large onion, finely chopped
2 garlic cloves, crushed
2 large carrots
400g beef stewing steak, in rough chunks

200g chopped tomatoes
150ml beef stock
1 tsp. dried oregano
1 tbsp. fresh chopped basil leaves

- ♥ Heat the oil in a large, heavy-bottomed saucepan.
- ♥ Add the onion and cook on a medium heat, stirring occasionally, until softened.
- ♥ Add the garlic and cook for a further 2 minutes.
- ♥ Add the beef and cook, stirring occasionally until brown on all sides.
- ♥ Add the carrots, beef stock, tomatoes and oregano, stirring until well-combined.

- ♥ Place a lid on top of the saucepan and simmer on low heat for 1–11/2 hours. If the stew is too liquid toward the end of the cooking time, remove the lid for about 10 minutes to allow some liquid to evaporate.
- ♥ Stir in the basil before serving.

Spicy Lamb Vindaloo

Serves: **5**

 Slimbites: **9**

For the marinade:
2 tbsp. cider vinegar
2 tbsp. olive oil
1/2 tsp. sea salt

For the lamb:
450g lamb shoulder meat, cut into 4cm chunks
1 tbsp. of cider vinegar
1 tbsp. olive oil
1 tbsp. coconut oil
1 onion, finely sliced
3 garlic cloves, minced
1 tbsp. fresh grated ginger
1/2 tsp. ground mustard

1/2 tsp. ground cumin
1 tsp. turmeric
1 tsp. cayenne pepper
1/2 tsp. red pepper flakes
1/2 tsp. ground coriander
1 tsp. paprika
1/2 tsp. ground cinnamon
4 tbsp. tomato paste
1 large tomato, diced
240ml lamb stock
1 bay leaf
sweet potatoes, cut into 2.5cm cubes
sea salt, to taste
black pepper, to taste

♥ Whisk together the cider vinegar, olive oil and sea salt in a large bowl to make the marinade. Add the lamb chunks and toss to completely coat the meat.

♥ Cover with plastic wrap and place in the refrigerator to marinate, preferably overnight or for at least 8 hours.

♥ Preheat the oven to 175°C/fan 165°C/gas 5.

♥ Heat the coconut oil in an oven-safe frying pan over a medium-high heat. Remove the lamb from the marinade and place in the hot pan. Cook the lamb for about 2–3 minutes per side.

♥ Once the lamb is browned, remove from the pan and set aside.

♥ Add the sliced onion to the same pan. Reduce heat to medium-low and sauté onions until they begin to brown (about 8–10 minutes).

♥ While the onions are sautéing, place the onion, garlic, olive oil, fresh ginger, ground mustard, ground cumin, turmeric, cayenne pepper, red pepper flake, ground coriander, paprika, and ground cinnamon in a food processor. Puree until smooth.

♥ Once the onions have browned, add the puree mixture to the pan. Cook for 2–3 minutes, until the spices become fragrant.

♥ Add the tomato paste and diced tomato. Continue to cook for another 2–3 minutes, stirring constantly to prevent burning. Add the lamb stock and stir until the ingredients are well combined.

♥ Add the lamb, 1 tablespoon of cider vinegar, a bay leaf, and sweet potatoes, and season with salt and pepper.

♥ Place the entire frying pan in the oven and bake for 60 minutes, until the lamb is tender.

♥ Remove from the oven and serve.

Lamb Koftas served with Cauliflower, Carrot and Parsnip Puree

Serves: 4 (two lamb koftas per person)

♥ **Slimbites: 10**

For the koftas:
1kg minced lamb
a handful of mint
a handful of coriander
1 tbsp. cinnamon
3 large cloves of garlic
2 tsp. ground cumin

For the puree:
4 tbsp. coconut butter
2 medium parsnips, coarsely chopped
2 large carrots, coarsely chopped
florets from 1 small head of cauliflower, chopped
4 garlic cloves
1/2 onion, coarsely chopped
120ml organic chicken broth
120ml water
kosher salt, to taste
freshly ground pepper, to taste

♥ For the koftas, mash all the ingredients and season with salt and pepper. Wet your hands and shape the meat into 16 small balls, place them on a hot griddle pan, turn them once and place them on to a skewer.

♥ For the puree, melt three tablespoons of coconut butter in a large stockpot over a medium heat and chop the veggies. Put the veggies, broth, and water into the pot and bring to a boil.

♥ Lower the heat and simmer in the covered pot for 25–30 minutes until the vegetables are mushy. Add salt, pepper, and the last tablespoon of coconut butter. Puree everything with an immersion blender.

♥ Serve koftas alongside the puree and a salad.

Individual Lamb Hot Pots

Serves: **2**

 Slimbites: **8**

1 tsp. coconut oil
220g lamb shoulder, cut into cubes
salt and pepper to season
1 onion, chopped
2 carrots, chopped
2 cloves garlic, minced
2 tsp. coconut flour
1 tbsp. Tamari

240ml lamb stock
4 sprigs fresh thyme, leaves removed
2 bay leaves
150g sweet potato, sliced thinly
1 tbsp. olive oil
sea salt, to taste
black pepper, to taste

- ♥ Preheat oven to 175°C/fan 155°C/gas 4.
- ♥ Heat the coconut oil in a frying pan over a medium heat.
- ♥ Season the lamb with salt and pepper and place in the frying pan.
- ♥ Brown the lamb on both sides, about 3–4 minutes per side.
- ♥ Once the lamb is browned, remove from the pan and set aside.
- ♥ Add the onions and carrots to the frying pan. Sauté the vegetables for 5 minutes until the onions become translucent. Add the garlic and cook for another 1–2 minutes.
- ♥ Sprinkle the coconut flour over the vegetables and cook while stirring constantly for 1–2 minutes.
- ♥ Add the Tamari and lamb stock.
- ♥ Use a wooden spoon to scrape the cooked bits off the bottom of the pan, forming gravy.
- ♥ Add in the fresh thyme.
- ♥ Divide the cooked lamb between the two individual baking dishes.
- ♥ Pour the vegetable and gravy mixture over the lamb, dividing evenly.
- ♥ Add a bay leaf to each dish.
- ♥ Take the sliced sweet potato and cover the top of each dish, overlapping the slices in a decorative pattern.
- ♥ Drizzle the sweet potatoes with olive oil and season with salt and pepper.
- ♥ Cover each baking dish with aluminium foil and bake in the preheated oven for 30 minutes.
- ♥ Remove the aluminium foil and bake for an additional 30 minutes, until the sweet potatoes are crispy.
- ♥ Remove from the oven and rest for 10 minutes before serving.

Asian Sea Bass with Courgette Noodles

Serves: **1**

♥ Slimbites: **6**

1 sea bass, scaled and cleaned
2 garlic cloves, diced
3–4 parsley stalks
1/4 tsp. fresh chopped ginger
3–4 spring onions, chopped
1 tsp. lemon zest
2 tbsp. lemon juice
1 small hot pepper

1 tbsp. olive oil
1 large courgette
1 small carrot
1/4 small onion
1 small red pepper
1 tsp. apple cider vinegar
salt and pepper to season
chopped spring onions and hot chilli, to serve

♥ Preheat the oven to 180°C/fan 160°C/gas 4.
♥ Mix the lemon juice, zest, diced garlic, hot pepper and ginger with a pinch of salt and rub mixture all over the fish. Place the parsley and one spring onion stalk into the fish cavity and secure with a toothpick.
♥ Wrap fish in foil and place into the oven for 20 minutes.
♥ Meanwhile with a knife cut the carrot, white onion and pepper into thin strips and use a spiralizer to noodle the courgette.

♥ Fry the onion, carrot and pepper strips in heated olive oil for 3–4 minutes. Then add the courgette noodles and mixture of vinegar and salt. Sauté the vegetable noodles until softened.
♥ To serve, sprinkle the fish with remaining chopped spring onions and hot chilli.

Top Tip: Spiralizers are a great way to keep your carbohydrate intake down. I actually prefer making pasta from my vegetables now as I find regular pasta too heavy and not filling enough; plus vegetable pasta obviously has a lot more nutrients and minerals.

Fish Stew with Chickpeas

Serves: **4**

 Slimbites: **5**

4 fillets of sea bass, scaled and cleaned
1 can chickpeas, drained and rinsed
1 can chopped tomatoes (sugar-free)
240ml vegetable broth
3 small garlic cloves, minced
1 medium red pepper, sliced into half rings
1 medium onion, chopped

2 tbsp. olive oil
1 tbsp. sweet paprika
1 tsp. lemon zest
1 tsp. fennel seeds
1/2 tsp. cumin seeds
salt to taste

♥ Sauté onion and pepper half rings for about 2–3 minutes. Add the minced garlic, zest and spices.
♥ Mix vegetables with the vegetable broth and canned tomatoes and let the sauce simmer for 8 minutes. Add chickpeas and cook for a couple of minutes more.
♥ Place the whole fish into the sauce, cover and stew for 20 minutes.
♥ Take fish fillets off the bones and place back into the sauce. To serve, sprinkle with chopped parsley and more lemon zest.

Fish Tagine

Serves: **2**

 Slimbites: **5**

1 small red onion
1 medium pepper
2 tbsp. olive oil
3 small garlic cloves, minced
1 tsp. chopped chilli pepper
120ml water
1/2 salted preserved lemon
1 tbsp. capers
200ml passata, unseasoned
1 tbsp. smoked paprika

1/2 tsp. dried thyme
1/2 tsp. rosemary
1/2 tsp. basil
1/2 tsp. tarragon
1/2 tsp. ground nutmeg
200g cleaned squid tubes
4 cod fillets
6–8 green olives
1 tbsp. chopped coriander

♥ Cut onion and pepper into thin strips and fry with the olive oil for 2–3 minutes. Add the minced garlic and chilli.

♥ Mix the vegetables with water, salted lemons (chopped zest and pulp), capers and passata, then sprinkle on paprika, dried herbs and nutmeg. Let the sauce simmer for 15 minutes on a low heat.

♥ Cut the squid tubes into 1cm rings and add them to the sauce with whole fish fillets, making sure that the fish is covered with the sauce.

♥ Cook for 3 minutes or until calamari turns opaque. Serve with some green olives and chopped coriander on top.

Coconut Crusted Fish Fingers

Serves: **2**

 Slimbites: **9**

350g white fish fillet
2/3 cup shredded coconut
citrus zest
30g chickpea flour
1/4 tsp. chilli powder

1/4 tsp. ground ginger
1 tsp. salt
1 egg
lemon slices

♥ Preheat the oven to 200°C/fan 180°C/gas 6.
♥ Mix the coconut with citrus zest and spices.
  Fry in a dry hot pan until coconut flakes turn a
  light cream colour.
♥ Cut the fish fillet into 2cm strips and sprinkle
  with salt.
♥ Beat the egg. Cover fish strips in flour and dip
  into beaten egg.
♥ Toss the fish fingers in coconut flakes and
  place onto a baking sheet.
♥ Bake for 20–22 minutes. Serve with a few extra
  lemon slices.

Spicy Scotch Eggs with Baked Sweet Potato Chips

Serves: **3**

 Slimbites: **8**

For scotch eggs:
360g minced pork
3 eggs (hard or soft boiled)
1 tsp. garlic powder
1 tsp. sweet paprika
1 tsp. dried tomatoes, minced
1 chilli pepper, finely chopped
sea salt, to taste

For sweet potato chips:
1 sweet potato
1 tbsp. olive oil
1 tsp. dried oregano
1 tsp. smoked paprika
sea salt, to taste

♥ Preheat the oven to 180°C/fan 160°C/gas 4. For the scotch eggs, mix the minced pork with the garlic, paprika and dried tomatoes, add the chopped chilli pepper and sea salt to taste. For this recipe you can also use pre-made pork sausage or pork mince combined with lean beef.
♥ Carefully peel the boiled eggs.
♥ Take 1/3 of the pork mince and flatten it between your palms to form a circular patty. Place boiled egg in the middle of pork patty and shape the mince all around the egg, trying to seal all of the empty spots and cracks. Repeat with the other two eggs.
♥ Put the moulded eggs in a greased muffin tin (one per hole) or straight onto a baking pan. Place the scotch eggs in the oven for 25–30 minutes.

♥ For the sweet potato chips, turn the oven up to 230°C/fan 210°C/gas 8. Peel and chop the sweet potato into chips (about 1–2cm thick). Mix the chopped potatoes with olive oil, salt, paprika, and oregano. Spread chips all over the greased baking dish, making sure they are not touching each other, and place into the oven for 30 minutes or till brown and crispy.

Snacks & Sauces

It is important when eating a Clean and Green diet, that you don't go hungry, because you may get what I call the wandering hand. This is where you pick up anything, whether it is good or bad and eat it just because you're hungry. If you work in an office environment like me, it's great to have healthy snacks to munch on throughout the day so that you don't end up buying a pastry from the local café or munching on the chocolate at the receptionist's desk. These Clean and Green snacks are so gorgeous your workmates will be jealous and are also perfect for your kid's lunch boxes to keep them energised all day.

The same goes for sauces. There are lots of sneaky sugars in shop-bought sauces; this is why it's good to make your own and keep in the fridge for later. Sauces take literally minutes to make and at least you know all the ingredients being added. Here are some of my favourite – 100 per cent natural – snacks and sauces… enjoy!

Almond Butter Date Balls

Serves: **8 (1 ball per serving)**    Slimbites: **3**

175g Medjool dates, pitted
185g almond butter
2 tbsp. slivered almonds, chopped

♥ In a food processor combine the dates and
   almond butter.
♥ Remove the mixture from the food processor
   and form it into 8 balls.
♥ Roll the balls in the chopped almonds.
♥ Refrigerate the balls until ready to serve.

Almond Butter Apple Stack

Serves: **2**

♥ Slimbites: **3**

1 apple
2 tbsp. almond butter

- ♥ Core the apple.
- ♥ Cut it into six even doughnut-shaped slices.
- ♥ Spread almond butter on two apple slices, then stack another on top.
- ♥ Add almond butter to the remaining two apple slices. Place one on each of the apple stacks, with the almond butter down.
- ♥ Serve immediately.

Top Tip: These are the simplest desserts ever made but the most delicious. To prevent browning, put the apple slices in iced water for 1–2 minutes.

Banana Egg Muffins

Serves: **4**

 Slimbites: **2**

1 ripe banana, mashed
2 eggs
1/4 tsp. ground cinnamon
a pinch of ground nutmeg
1 tbsp. almonds, slivered

♥ Preheat oven to 190°C/fan 170°C/gas 5.
♥ In a large mixing bowl, combine the
  mashed banana, eggs, ground cinnamon
  and ground nutmeg.
♥ Use an electric mixer to beat the banana egg
  mixture until smooth.
♥ Fold in the slivered almonds.
♥ Pour the mixture into muffin tins lined with
  cupcake liners.
♥ Bake for 10–15 minutes, until muffins are
  cooked through.
♥ Remove from the muffin tins and let cool.

Chicken Bacon Bites

Serves: **6**

 Slimbites: **3**

1 tsp. ground cinnamon
1/2 tsp. smoked paprika
1/2 tsp. cayenne pepper
1 tsp. garlic powder

sea salt and freshly ground black pepper, to taste
2 rashers of bacon
2 chicken breasts cut into bite size pieces

- Preheat the oven to 200°C/fan 180°C/gas 4 and line a large baking tray with foil.
- In a bowl, add cinnamon, paprika, cayenne pepper, garlic powder, salt and black pepper and mix till thoroughly combined. Set aside.
- Slice the bacon strips and chicken breasts into small bite-size pieces.
- Wrap the chicken pieces with bacon slices using a toothpick to secure the bacon onto the chicken.

- Rub all the bacon wrapped pieces with spice mixture generously.
- Arrange all bacon-wrapped pieces into prepared baking dish in a single layer.
- Bake for about 25–30 minutes.

Avocado Chicken Cups

Serves: **2**

 Slimbites: **1**

1 large cucumber
1 lemon
1 ripe avocado, pitted
200g cooked chicken, shredded (leftover roast chicken is perfect!)

1/2 large red pepper, seeded and diced
salt, to taste
black pepper, to taste

- ♥ Cut the cucumber into 8 equal pieces.
- ♥ Use a spoon to scoop out half the insides of each piece of cucumber to fit the chicken and avocado mix in. So you are making little cucumber cups.
- ♥ Place the cucumber cups on a plate and set aside.
- ♥ In a large bowl, mash together the avocado and lemon juice.
- ♥ Add the cooked shredded chicken and red bell pepper and stir until ingredients are well combined.

- ♥ Season with salt and pepper to taste.
- ♥ Spoon the chicken mixture into the cucumber cups, dividing equally.
- ♥ Enjoy!

Buffalo Chicken Wings

Serves: **4**

 Slimbites: **7**

675g chicken wings
2 tbsp. almond butter
4 tbsp. hot pepper sauce (with no added sugar
or preservatives)
2 tsp. extra-virgin olive oil
1/4 tsp. rock salt

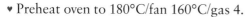

- ♥ Preheat oven to 180°C/fan 160°C/gas 4.
- ♥ Line a rimmed baking sheet with greaseproof paper and spread the wings out evenly onto the sheet. Bake for 20 minutes.
- ♥ Meanwhile, soften almond butter in a small saucepan over a medium heat. Stir occasionally.
- ♥ When soft, stir in hot pepper sauce, olive oil, and salt. If sauce gets too thick, add a bit of hot water.

- ♥ After 20 minutes of cooking, remove wings from oven. Turn each wing over and brush the upward facing side of each wing with sauce. Return to oven for 10 more minutes.
- ♥ Turn each wing to the other side, baste that side with sauce, and return to oven for 10 additional minutes (or until completely cooked).
- ♥ Serve and enjoy.

Chocolate Banana Cookies

Serves: **5**

 Slimbites: **3**

2 ripe bananas, mashed
2 tbsp. almond butter
2 tbsp. cocoa powder
2 tsp. vanilla extract

1 tsp. baking powder
a pinch of salt
120g almond flour
1/4 tsp. stevia

♥ Preheat oven to 175°C/fan 155°C/gas 4.
♥ In a large bowl, combine all ingredients, mixing until a batter forms.
♥ Spoon 1 heaped tablespoon of the batter onto a baking sheet for each cookie.
♥ Bake in the oven for 8–10 minutes.
♥ Remove from the baking sheet and allow to cool on a wire rack before serving.

Courgette Fritters

Serves: **5–6**

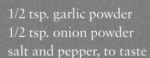 Slimbites: **4**

2 large courgettes
2 eggs
1 spring onion, finely chopped
30g coconut flour
1 tbsp. potato flour (gluten-free)

1/2 tsp. garlic powder
1/2 tsp. onion powder
salt and pepper, to taste
4 tbsp. olive oil

♥ Coarsely grate the courgette into a large bowl. Mix in 2 tablespoons of salt. Leave to sit for 10 minutes to sweat out excess water.

♥ After 10 minutes, place the courgette into a clean tea towel and squeeze out all the excess water. There will be a lot.

♥ Place courgette back into a large mixing bowl and combine with the egg, almond flour, spring onion and seasonings.

♥ Heat 2 tablespoons of olive oil in a large deep frying pan.

♥ With wet hands, form patty shapes out of the courgette mixture.

♥ Drop them into the frying pan three at a time and cook over a low to medium heat for 3–4 minutes and then turn and cook for a further 3–4 minutes until browned and cooked through.

♥ Serve on a bed of lettuce.

Ginger Snap Date Bars (Lara Bars)

Serves: **12 bars (1 bar per serving)**

 Slimbites: **2**

130g dates, coarsely chopped
1 tbsp. fresh ginger
70g mixed almonds and pecans
pinch of ground cinnamon
pinch of ground cloves

- ♥ Add all the ingredients to a food processor or tabletop blender.
- ♥ Process for 2–3 minutes, or until the mixture is well ground but bits of nut remain visible.
- ♥ Line a square baking dish with parchment paper.
- ♥ Spread the date mixture into the prepared baking dish.
- ♥ Use the back of a spatula to press the date mixture down firm and into an even layer.
- ♥ Cover the dish with plastic wrap and place in the refrigerator for about 2 hours.

- ♥ Gently lift the parchment paper out of the dish and place on a flat surface.
- ♥ Using a sharp knife, cut into squares or bars.
- ♥ Wrap each bar in wax paper or parchment paper to prevent sticking.
- ♥ Store in an airtight container.

Plantain Crisps

Serves: **6**

 Slimbites: **3**

2 green plantains
1 tbsp. coconut oil

a pinch of salt

♥ Line a baking sheet with parchment paper. Preheat oven to 175°C/fan 155°C/gas 3 or 4.
♥ Score the peel, being careful not to pierce the plantain. Gently peel the green skin off.
♥ Cut the plantain into 6mm-thick crisps at a diagonal.
♥ Toss in coconut oil to coat.
♥ Place crisps in an even layer on the prepared baking sheet.
♥ Sprinkle with salt.

♥ Bake for 20–25 minutes, or until plantains are just beginning to brown.
♥ Store in an airtight container.

Prosciutto Crisps

Serves: **4**

 Slimbites: **1**

4 slices of prosciutto di parma

- ♥ Preheat the oven to 175°C/fan 155°C/gas 4.
- ♥ Prepare a large rimmed baking sheet with greaseproof paper.
- ♥ Tear or cut each slice of prosciutto into four pieces.
- ♥ Evenly arrange on the baking sheet.
- ♥ Bake in the oven for 12–15 minutes or until crispy.
- ♥ Move to a cooling rack.
- ♥ Store in an airtight container.

Prawn and Soft Flour Tortillas

Serves: **2**

 Slimbites: **3**

For the prawns:
4–6 medium prawns, deveined and peeled
1 lime
1 tsp. crushed red pepper flakes
salt and pepper, to taste
1 tsp. coconut oil
1 onion, sliced
1 pepper, sliced
1 garlic clove, finely chopped

For the tortillas:
5 egg whites
30g coconut flour
60ml unsweetened coconut or almond milk
1 tsp. cumin
1/2 tsp. chilli powder
1/4 tsp. sea salt
1/2 tsp. coconut oil

For the prawns:

♥ Put the egg whites, coconut flour, milk, cumin, chilli powder and salt into a blender or food processor.

♥ Process until well combined (it should come out quite thin). Set aside.

♥ Allow the batter to sit for 5–7 minutes.

♥ Meanwhile, add the prawns, lime juice and red pepper to a bowl. Toss to coat.

♥ Season with salt and pepper and place to one side.

♥ Heat a frying pan or cast iron pan over a medium-high heat. Add the coconut oil to the pan.

♥ Add the onion and bell pepper. Sauté for 3–4 minutes.

♥ Add the garlic and sauté for another 2–3 minutes.

♥ Finally, add the prawns. Sauté until they are pink and cooked through. Set the pan aside while you make the tortillas, cover to keep it warm.

For the tortillas:

♥ Place a small non-stick frying pan over a medium high heat.

♥ Add the coconut oil and move the pan around to make sure it covers the entire surface.

♥ Using a ladle, add 1/4 of the mixture to the hot frying pan.

♥ Lift it up and move it around to spread the batter around in a circle in the frying pan.

♥ Cook for 2–3 minutes on one side, until the exposed side is no longer shiny.

♥ Flip carefully, using a large spatula.

♥ Cook for another 1–2 minutes, or until browned.

♥ Remove and set to one side.

♥ Repeat with remaining batter to make 4 tortillas. Take care not to place them on top of each other or they'll stick to each other.

♥ Serve each person 2 tortillas to fill with prawns and peppers.

♥ Enjoy!

Balsamic Steak

Serves: **6**

 Slimbites: **4**

680g skirt steak, cut into strips
1 carrot, cut into small thin slices
1 pepper, cut into thin strips
1 courgette, julienned
1/2 tsp. dried oregano
1/2 tsp. dried basil
Sea salt and black pepper, to taste

For the balsamic:
1 tbsp. coconut oil
60ml balsamic vinegar
60ml beef stock
Sea salt and black pepper, to taste

♥ Preheat the oven to 180°C/fan 160°C/gas 4.
♥ Put the coconut oil in a saucepan and place it over a medium heat.
♥ Add the balsamic vinegar and beef stock to the pan. Season with salt and pepper to taste.
♥ Allow the mixture to simmer until it thickens. Remove from heat and set aside.
♥ Season the steak with salt, pepper, oregano and basil.
♥ Place the chopped vegetables into about 4–6 evenly distributed bundles.

♥ Tightly wrap the steak around the bundles (as if the vegetables were a flower bouquet and the steak is the ribbon), securing it with a wooden toothpick.
♥ Place the rolls on a baking sheet and bake for 10–12 minutes.
♥ Serve the steak rolls with the balsamic glaze.

Broccoli Sausage Bites

Serves: **8 bites**

 Slimbites: **4**

1 large head broccoli, cooked and chopped
260g sausage, casings removed
95g almond flour
1/2 tsp. garlic powder

1/2 tsp. ground mustard
1/2 tsp. onion powder
1 egg
salt

♥ Preheat oven to 190°C/fan 170°C/gas 4 or 5.
♥ In a large bowl, combine the chopped
broccoli, sausage, almond flour, garlic powder,
ground mustard, onion powder, egg and salt.
♥ Use your hands to mix the ingredients together.
♥ Form the mixture into 8 equal patties. Place
the patties on a baking sheet.
♥ Bake the patties in the oven for 15 minutes.
Flip the patties and bake for an additional
10–15 minutes, until cooked through.

Paleo Sweet and Spicy Nut Mix

Serves: **6**

 Slimbites: **0.5**

60g almonds, raw or roasted, unsalted
4 tbsp. sunflower seeds, hulled, raw or
   roasted, unsalted
pinch of chilli powder

pinch of paprika
1 tsp. salt
5 tbsp. unsweetened raisins

♥ Mix all the ingredients together in a bowl. Stir
to combine.
♥ Store in an airtight container.

Top Tip: I always keep a big stash in a jar in the cupboard to take to work for snacks. You can make all different trail mixes but this is definitely my favourite.

Avocado Tzatziki Dip

Serves: **4**　　　　　　　　　 Slimbites: **1**

1 avocado
1/4 onion
1 garlic clove
1 large peeled cucumber
1 lemon, juiced
1 tbsp. fresh mint

♥ Place all the ingredients in a food processor.
♥ Blend until smooth.
♥ Serve with carrots, or sliced green and red
  bell pepper.

Sugar-free Ketchup

 Slimbites: **0.2 (per serving)**

1 can of unsweetened tomato paste
80ml water
2 tbsp. vinegar

1 tbsp. lemon juice
1 tsp. chopped garlic
1 tsp. salt
1 tsp. cayenne pepper

- ♥ Mix all ingredients in a saucepan and bring to boil on a medium-high heat.
- ♥ Reduce heat to medium-low and simmer while stirring frequently until flavours have blended (add more water for thinner ketchup, add less water for thicker).
- ♥ Transfer to a glass jar and cool before serving.
- ♥ Keep chilled and in the fridge.

Mayo

 Slimbites: **2 (per serving)**

2 eggs
2–3 tsp. fresh lemon

1/4 tsp. Himalayan salt
240ml extra light tasting olive oil

♥ Add all the ingredients to a glass jar and let them sit for a few seconds, just long enough for the egg to settle comfortably at the bottom of the jar, underneath the oil.

♥ Insert an immersion blender and push it all the way down until it makes contact with the bottom of the jar.

♥ Push the power button and do not move the blender for a full 20 seconds. Almost instantly, the oil will start to emulsify and turn into a lusciously creamy and thick concoction.

♥ After 20 seconds, start moving the blender around and up and down just to make sure that every last bit of oil is incorporated.

♥ Store in the refrigerator in an airtight container for up to 2 weeks.

Pumpkin Applesauce

 Slimbites: **1.5 (per serving)**

Half a small sugar pumpkin (the smaller
   pumpkins – known as sugar pumpkins –
   are sweeter)
4 apples, cored, peeled and chopped
pinch of ground cinnamon
pinch of ground nutmeg

- Preheat the oven to 175°C/fan 155°C/gas 3 or 4.
- Place the apples in a baking dish, sprinkle with
  cinnamon and nutmeg. Cover with foil.
- Cut off the top of the pumpkin.
- Place the pumpkin on a baking sheet, flesh
  side up, skin side down.
- Place both in the preheated oven.
- Cook the apples for up to 20 minutes, or until
  soft. For a chunkier applesauce, only cook for
  10–15 minutes. Remove and set aside.
- Cook the pumpkin for 45 minutes to an hour,
  until tender. The smell is delicious – it's just
  like baking cookies!
- Scoop out the pumpkin, discarding the skin.
- Place the apples and pumpkin flesh in a blender
  or food processor. Process until you reach the
  desired consistency. An immersion blender
  could also be used to process the applesauce.
- Chill in the refrigerator, if desired.
- Store in an airtight container.

Top Tip: I am always talking about this dish to yummy mummies with toddlers – with no added sugar it's perfect to get toddlers started in life! The sauce is also ideal for a sweet treat on top of fruit or even as a sweet and sour dish. It's full of nutrients and minerals and high in vitamin A.

Dessert

Now it's time for my favourite part of the book… the desserts! I have always had a sweet tooth but it's not as sweet as it used to be. I can honestly say I didn't know what an apple tasted like until I was 24; prior to that I had been eating sugar processed foods and my taste buds had died under my very nose. Now I stay away from processed foods and processed sugar, and stick with the natural stuff. I can taste all the flavours and the thought of even having a sip of Coke now makes me cringe as it tastes like syrupy sick. After 21 days of eating Clean and Green your taste buds will come back to life!

You will find that these desserts are crammed with natural good fats and natural sugars full of vitamin and minerals. I have chosen to use three sorts of sugar. Sugar from fruits; date sugar because it is the healthiest sugar in the world and full of antioxidants; and stevia because it is unique in that it's made naturally, does not have a GI index and does not spike your insulin levels. If you are going to have a sweet treat have a good one not a bad one. Your body is the most unique, clever, beautifully designed piece of engineering you are ever going to own, be good to it.

Almond Butter and Jelly Ice Cream

Serves: **9**

 Slimbites: **6**

2 cans of full-fat coconut milk
1 tsp. of powdered stevia
125g almond butter
75g partially thawed frozen strawberries

♥ Empty the two cans of coconut milk in a large
  bowl and whisk in the stevia until well mixed.
♥ Mix in the almond butter, combining with an
  electric whisk.
♥ Put the mixture into the freezer for about
  6 hours.
♥ Once frozen, place into a food processor to
  smooth the mixture.
♥ Smash the partially thawed frozen strawberries
  and fold into the ice cream mixture.
♥ You can freeze for another 2 hours or simply
  enjoy as is.

Baked Apples and Cinnamon

Serves: **4**

 Slimbites: **3.5**

6 large apples
120g walnuts, coarsely chopped
1/2 tbsp. powdered stevia (optional)
1/2 tsp. vanilla extract

2 tbsp. powdered cinnamon (bear in mind
  I love cinnamon! Feel free to use less.)
4 cinnamon sticks (optional)

♥ Preheat oven to 190°C/fan 170°C/gas 5.
♥ Cut off about a 1cm from the top of each of
  the 4 apples (keep the tops).
♥ Scoop out the insides from four of the apples,
  leaving the walls about 5mm thick. Be careful
  not to break the skin (a melon baller works
  great for this).
♥ Skin the two remaining apples, and then chop
  them into little cubes.
♥ In a bowl, combine the cubed apples, walnuts,
  cinnamon and stevia.
♥ Scoop the apple mixture into the 4 hollowed-
  out apples.
♥ Put the tops of the apples back on. You can
  use a cinnamon stick to hold the apple top
  securely in place.

♥ Place the stuffed apples in a small roasting
  pan. Add some water to cover the bottom of
  the pan.
♥ Cover the pan and apples with foil and bake
  for 25 minutes.
♥ Remove the foil and bake for an additional
  15 minutes.
♥ Cool for 5 minutes and serve.

Baked Peaches and Coconut Cream

Serves: **4**

 Slimbites: **3**

For the peaches:
4 large, ripe peaches
4 tbsp. coconut oil melted and cooled to
    room temp
1/2 tbsp. powdered stevia (optional)
1/2 tsp. vanilla extract
2 tsp. cinnamon
squeeze of lemon juice

For the whipped coconut cream:
1 can full-fat coconut cream, refrigerated
    overnight
1/2 tbsp. powdered stevia
1 tsp. vanilla extract

♥ Preheat the oven to 180°C/fan 160°C/gas 4.
♥ Melt the coconut oil and leave it at room
  temperature to cool down. Add the stevia,
  vanilla extract, cinnamon and lemon juice.
  Mix to combine.
♥ Slice the peaches in half. Remove the pits and
  place the peaches cut side up in a baking dish.
♥ Pour the coconut oil mixture over the peaches,
  saving a little bit for basting the peaches later
  during baking.
♥ Place in the preheated oven and bake for
  approximately 35 minutes or until the peaches
  are tender. Baste the peaches with the syrup a
  couple of times during baking.
♥ Remove from the oven and let cool.

♥ For the whipped cream: open the can of
  coconut cream and scoop just the thick, fatty
  layer of coconut cream off the top and place
  in a bowl. Beat the coconut cream by hand or
  with a mixer until smooth. Add the stevia and
  vanilla and beat for another 1–2 minutes until
  the mixture is light and creamy. If you prefer,
  you can make the cream ahead of time and
  store it in the fridge.
♥ Serve the peaches with the coconut cream.

Banana and Walnut Ice Cream

Serves: **2**

 Slimbites: **5**

2 medium frozen bananas
70g walnuts
60ml unsweetened vanilla almond milk
 (or other non-dairy milk)
60ml unsweetened coconut milk
a pinch of cinnamon
1/2 tsp. vanilla extract

♥ Combine all ingredients in a high-speed
 blender or food processor and blend until
 thick and creamy.
♥ Serve as is or freeze for 1–2 hours to create
 a harder consistency.
♥ Top with more walnut chunks and serve
 between a sliced banana.

Chia Seed Chocolate Pudding

Serves: **4**

 Slimbites: **2**

360ml almond milk (or other non-dairy
   milk)
5 1/2 tbsp. chia seeds
4 tbsp. unsweetened cocoa powder
1 tbsp. powdered stevia
1/2 tsp. cinnamon
1/2 tsp. vanilla extract

♥ Add all the ingredients together in a mixing
   bowl and whisk to combine.
♥ Rest the mixture in the fridge for 3 to 5 hours.
♥ Serve chilled with desired toppings such as
   fruit, nuts or whipped coconut cream.

Coconut Banana Bread

Serves: **10**

 Slimbites: **4**

8 tbsp. coconut oil, melted and cooled
1/2 tbsp. powdered stevia
1/2 tsp. of sea salt
6 eggs
2 tsp. vanilla extract

1 tsp. almond extract
125g coconut flour
2 medium bananas, mashed
unsweetened shredded coconut, for garnish

♥ Preheat oven to 190°C/fan 170°C/gas 5.
♥ Grease a loaf pan with some coconut oil.
♥ In a small bowl, combine coconut oil and stevia. Set aside.
♥ In a large bowl, whisk the eggs, vanilla extract, and the salt and almond extract together.
♥ Combine the coconut oil and stevia mixture into the egg mixture, whisking thoroughly.
♥ Whisk in the coconut flour, making sure it is completely combined.

♥ Lastly, stir in the mashed bananas.
♥ Pour the batter into the loaf pan and cover with shredded coconut.
♥ Cover with foil and bake for 40 minutes.
♥ Remove the foil and cook for another 10 to 15 minutes or until the top browns.
♥ Cool and keep refrigerated.

Coconut Lime Date Balls

Serves: **13**

 Slimbites: **2**

85g slivered almonds
200g Medjool dates, pitted
juice and zest of 2 limes
1/4 cup unsweetened shredded coconut

♥ Add the almonds to a food processor and
  pulse until they are finely chopped.
♥ Add the dates, lime zest, and lime juice to the
  food processor. Pulse until a clumpy paste
  forms (there should still be chunks of nuts
  in the paste).
♥ Remove the paste from the food processor.
♥ Use your hands to form the paste into 13
  equal-sized balls.
♥ Pour the shredded coconut out on a flat surface.
♥ Roll the balls in the coconut, until they
  are covered.
♥ Store the balls in the refrigerator until ready
  to serve.

Sugar-Free Coffee Brownies

Serves: **9**

 Slimbites: **4**

1 egg
1/2 tbsp. powdered stevia
2 tbsp. coconut oil
1 tsp. vanilla extract
120ml strong coffee
260g almond butter (another nut/seed butter
  would also work)

28g coconut flour, sifted to remove lumps
3 tbsp. cocoa powder
2 tbsp. ground coffee
1/2 tsp. baking soda
1/4 tsp. salt

♥ Preheat the oven to 180°C/160°F/gas 4.
♥ In a large bowl, whisk the egg and add the stevia,
  coconut oil, vanilla extract and brewed coffee.
♥ Mix in the almond butter.
♥ In a separate bowl, add the sifted coconut
  flour, cocoa powder, ground coffee, baking
  soda and salt, and mix thoroughly.
♥ Add the coconut flour mixture to the egg
  and almond butter mixture. Mix thoroughly.

♥ Grease a 20cm x 20cm glass baking dish with
  coconut oil. Pour the brownie mixture
  into the dish.
♥ Bake for 25 to 30 minutes.
♥ Cool a little after baking and then cut
  into 9 squares.

Sweet Date Syrup

 Slimbites: **4**

350g seedless/pitted dates
480ml water

♥ Put the water in a small pan and bring to a boil.

♥ Wash the dates and place them in a large bowl.

♥ Take the water off the heat and pour it into the bowl with the dates. Soak for 2 hours.

♥ Leaving the dates in the water, use a masher to mash them up thoroughly.

♥ Place a colander over a large pot and line the colander with cheesecloth.

♥ Pour the mashed dates into the colander, filtering out the water. Squeeze the pulp through the cheesecloth to ensure all the water is removed.

♥ Remove the pulp inside the cheesecloth and put it back into the original soaking bowl with a little more hot water, mash it and filter it back into the colander through the cheesecloth.

♥ Remove the colander from the pan. You should be left with an amber coloured liquid in the bottom of the pan.

♥ Set the liquid over a medium high heat and bring it to a boil, continuously stirring to prevent sticking. Continue boiling for about 10 minutes, until the liquid becomes thick like honey.

♥ Remove from the heat and pour into a glass jar to store. Keep sealed and refrigerated.

Lemon 'Cheese' Cake

Serves: **7**

 Slimbites: **12**

For the crust:
125g pecans
70g almonds
75g hazelnuts
6 Medjool dates, pitted and soaked for
   45 minutes
2 tbsp. coconut flakes

For the filling:
300g raw cashews, soaked for 4 or more hours
240ml coconut cream, refrigerated overnight
1 and 1/2 tbsp. powdered stevia
1 tbsp. lemon zest
3 tbsp. lemon juice
pinch of salt

To make the crust:
♥ Grease a shallow 20cm x 20cm tin with
  coconut oil.
♥ Combine all nuts in a food processor and
  process until fine.
♥ Add in the dates and coconut flakes,
  processing until coarse crumble starts to form.
♥ Evenly spread the crust dough in a pie tin with
  your fingers until it covers the bottom and fills
  half the tin.

To make the filling:
♥ Drain the soaked cashews.
♥ Pour the coconut cream, soaked cashews and
  remaining ingredients into a food processor.
♥ Blend on high until completely creamy.
♥ Pour filling into crust and spread out evenly.
♥ Chill until set – about 3–4 hours in the fridge.
♥ Top with desired fresh fruit.

Good for You Tiramisu

Serves: **2-4**

 Slimbites: **5.5**

Base and centre layer:
115g peeled hazelnuts
95g pecans
80g coconut flour
70g almonds
90g Medjool dates, pitted and
    soaked in cool water for 45 minutes
3 tbsp. coconut oil, melted and cooled to
    room temperature

Coffee cream layer:
45g Medjool dates, pitted and soaked in
    cool water for 45 minutes
1/2 can full-fat coconut milk
70g raw cacao butter
2 tsp. raw cacao powder
1/2 tsp. vanilla extract
2 shots of espresso, cooled to room temperature
2 tbsp. coconut oil, melted and cooled to
room temperature

Cream layer:
150g raw cashews soaked for at least 4 hours
60ml full-fat coconut milk
60ml coconut oil, melted and cooled to room temp
2 tbsp. date syrup
1/2 tsp. vanilla extract
2 tbsp. unsweetened cocoa powder

Base and centre layer:
♥ Drain the water from the dates and discard
  the water. Blend the dates into a paste in a
  food processor. Remove and set aside.
♥ Blend the hazelnuts with the pecans until coarse
  and crumbly. Return the dates, along with the
  almonds, coconut flour and melted coconut oil
  to the food processor. Blend together.

♥ Place half of the mix in to an 20cm x 20cm
  pan, lined with parchment paper.
♥ Spread evenly along the bottom and press
  down to compact.
♥ Place in the fridge while you make the coffee
  cream layer. Set the remainder of the base
  mixture to one side at room temperature.

Coffee cream layer:

♥ Blend dates to a paste in a food processor. Add in coconut milk and blend to combine.

♥ Add all other ingredients for this layer and process until smooth.

♥ Remove the base from the fridge and pour the coffee cream over the top.

♥ Take the leftover mixture from the base and crumble it evenly onto the coffee cream layer.

♥ Return the pan to the fridge while you make the topping.

Cream layer:

♥ Blend the soaked and drained cashews with coconut milk in a food processor until smooth. Combine all other ingredients and blend.

♥ Pour over the second base layer. Gently spread to ensure it's even.

♥ Return to the fridge to set overnight or for a minimum of 4 hours.

♥ Slice into 9 squares and dust with unsweetened cocoa powder. Serve and enjoy!

Paleo Bounty Bars

Serves: **9**

240ml coconut oil
1/2 can full-fat coconut milk
40g desiccated coconut
1 vanilla bean

 Slimbites: **6**

1 tbsp. coconut flour
55g cacao powder
60ml unrefined coconut oil liquid
4–5 drops liquid stevia, to taste

♥ Heat the coconut oil and coconut milk over a low heat. Heat until melted and whisk continuously to combine.

♥ Stir in the desiccated coconut.

♥ Cut the vanilla bean lengthwise down the centre. Slit it open and carefully scrape the seeds out using the back of a knife. Add the seeds to the mixture and discard the pod. Stir to combine.

♥ Add the coconut flour, whisking until the mixture resembles porridge.

♥ Set aside to hydrate and cool slightly (approximately 10 minutes).

♥ Transfer the coconut mixture to a bread or loaf pan. Spread it into an even layer about 2.5cm thick. Cover and place in the freezer overnight (or for at least 5 hours).

♥ Remove the coconut filling from the freezer and allow to sit at room temperature for about 20–25 minutes.

♥ Prepare the chocolate by combining the cacao powder, 4 tbsp. coconut oil, and stevia in a bowl. Whisk to combine until the mixture resembles melted chocolate. Set aside.

♥ Once the coconut filling has finished setting, remove from the freezer and cut into 9 evenly shaped bars.

♥ Dip each bar into the chocolate, completely coating the surface. Set aside on wax paper.

♥ Put the dipped coconut bars into the freezer to set.

♥ Store bars in the freezer, as the chocolate will melt at room temperature.

Homemade Custard

 Slimbites: **3.5**

480ml coconut milk
2 eggs
2 tsp. vanilla extract
2 tbsp. date syrup

♥ Heat the coconut milk in a saucepan with vanilla extract and date syrup and bring to almost boiling point, then remove from the heat.

♥ Beat the eggs in a stainless steel mixing bowl until combined.

♥ Pour the hot milk over the eggs and whisk in well.

♥ Pour the egg mixture back into the saucepan and cook over a gentle heat, stirring with a wooden spoon until it thickens and coats the back of the spoon.

♥ Remove from the heat quickly and pour back into the mixing bowl. Whisk to cool a little and smooth it out. If you see any lumps then strain through a sieve.

♥ Serve hot or cold.

Pavlova

Serves: **6**

 Slimbites: **5**

Meringue base:
6 egg whites, at room temperature
120ml date syrup
1 tsp. lemon juice
2 tbsp. arrowroot powder
1/2 tsp. vanilla extract

Whipped coconut cream topping:
2 cans full-fat coconut cream, refrigerated
  overnight
1/2 tbsp. powdered stevia
1/2 tsp. vanilla extract
1/2 tsp. cinnamon
fresh fruit or berries

Base:
- Preheat oven to 135°C/fan 115°C/gas 1.
- You'll be using a double boiler method with a mixing bowl and a pot. In the pot that will hold your mixing bowl, bring 1–2 inches of water to a simmer.
- In the mixing bowl, first combine egg whites, date syrup, lemon juice and then set over the pot of simmering water, stirring until mixture is warm (for only about 2 minutes so the eggs don't cook!).
- Remove the bowl from the heat and using a whisk attachment on high speed, beat the mixture until it starts thickening. Add arrowroot powder and keep whipping until it reaches a stiff consistency. This usually takes about 10 minutes. The meringue mixture should be thick enough to maintain spoon-shaped peaks.
- Line a baking sheet with parchment paper. With a pencil, draw a circle on the parchment paper (an upside-down bowl works well). Spread the mixture onto the circle.
- Bake in the oven for 60–75 minutes, on the lowest rack. Check often. It should be a light golden brown colour.
- Remove from oven and let cool.

Topping:
- Scoop off the solid cream from the lid of the coconut cream can into a mixing bowl.
- Add stevia, cinnamon, and vanilla and whip on high speed until you see a thick, whipped cream-like consistency.
- Spread the whipped coconut cream onto the cooled meringue crust.
- Top with fresh fruits or berries of your choice.

No-bake Pumpkin Bars

Serves: **Makes 12 bars**

 Slimbites: **4**

10 pitted Medjool dates, soaked for 45 mins
110g almonds
1 and 1/2 tbsp. unsweetened cacao powder
2 tsp. cinnamon divided in half (1 tsp. each for
   two individual steps of the recipe)
55g unsweetened coconut flakes

1 tbsp. coconut oil, melted
1/2 tsp. vanilla extract
5 tbsp. pumpkin puree
1/2 of a medium banana
1/2 tbsp. powdered stevia

♥ Line a 23cm x 13cm pan with waxed paper.
♥ Place the almonds in a food processor and
   chop finely.
♥ Add the soaked dates, cocoa powder and first
   teaspoon of cinnamon to the almonds. Blend
   until a rough-looking dough starts to form.
♥ Transfer the dough to the pan and use a
   spatula to flatten it evenly.
♥ Place the coconut flakes, coconut oil and
   vanilla into the food processor and blend until
   a paste starts to form.

♥ Add to the pan and spread evenly over the
   almond base.
♥ Place the pumpkin puree, banana, stevia and
   the second teaspoon of cinnamon into the
   food processor and blend until smooth. Spread
   evenly on top of the coconut mixture.
♥ Sprinkle some coconut flakes on top.
♥ Place in the freezer for 1 to 2 hours.
♥ Cut into squares and serve.

Raspberry and Apple Crumble

Serves: **6**

 Slimbites: **7**

For the filling:
5 medium-sized apples, peeled, cored and diced
250g raspberries, frozen or fresh
1 tbsp. arrowroot powder

For the crumble:
110g sliced almonds
65g pecan pieces
85g ground flaxseeds
2 heaped tbsp. coconut flour
2 tbsp. coconut oil, softened
1/2 tbsp. powdered stevia

♥ Preheat oven to 190°C/fan 170°C/gas 5.
♥ To make the filling, mix up the apples, raspberries and arrowroot powder and spoon it into a large pan so it covers the bottom. Simmer for 30 minutes or until the apple chunks have softened. Then pour into a 23cm x 23cm dish or pie plate.
♥ For the crumble: using a food processor, grind the almonds, pecans and flaxseeds into a rough crumb. You want some larger pieces in there for variety but it should essentially be a grainy texture. Transfer this to a mixing bowl and stir in the coconut flour. Stir together the coconut oil and stevia before pouring into the nut mixture.

♥ Mix the crumble with the coconut oil and stevia until it starts to clump – it should resemble breadcrumbs.
♥ Spoon the crumble onto the fruit layer so that it is evenly distributed. Bake for 15 – 20 minutes.

Raw Chocolate Truffles

Serves: **4**

 Slimbites: **3**

6 dates, pitted and chopped
2 tbsp. almond butter
1 tsp. stevia
2 tbsp. softened coconut oil
2 tbsp. cacao powder (plus more for coating)
1 tsp. vanilla extract

♥ Add all the ingredients to a food processor.
♥ Blend until a paste forms.
♥ Transfer the mixture to a bowl and place in the refrigerator to cool for 30 minutes, until it sets.
♥ Divide the mixture into 8 pieces and roll each piece with your hands into a ball.
♥ Pour some additional cocoa powder onto a small plate or bowl. Roll each truffle in the cocoa powder, lightly dusting the outside.
♥ Place the finished truffles in a container and store in the refrigerator until ready to serve.

Raw Chocolate Bunnies

Serves: **3**

 Slimbites: **4**

20g cacao powder
4 tbsp. melted unrefined coconut oil
4–5 drops liquid stevia, to taste

♥ For this recipe you'll need a bunny-shaped
silicone chocolate mould, but you can
obviously use any mould of your choice!
♥ Add all ingredients to a bowl. Stir to combine.
♥ Pour the chocolate mixture into the mould,
filling each about halfway.
♥ Place the filled mould on a baking sheet.
♥ Lay the baking sheet on a flat surface in the
freezer for up to 20 minutes to set.
♥ Carefully pop the chocolate out of the mould.
♥ Place the chocolates in an airtight container
in the freezer to store as they will melt at
room temperature.

Simple Ice Lollies

Serves: **2**

 Slimbites: **1**

100g strawberries
50g grapes
75g raspberries
bamboo skewers

♥ Stick the fruit onto the skewer, in whatever combination you prefer. Lay flat on a plate and put in the freezer until frozen.

Sugar-Free Trifle

Serves: **2–3**

♥ Slimbites: **9**

Cake layer:

4 tbsp. coconut oil, melted and cooled to
    room temperature
1/2 tbsp. powdered stevia
1/2 tsp. sea salt
3 eggs
1 tsp. vanilla extract
1/2 tsp. almond extract
35g coconut flour
2 bananas, mashed

Coconut cream:

2 cans coconut cream – refrigerated overnight
2 tsp. vanilla extract
2 tsp. powdered stevia
200g sliced strawberries

Preparation:

♥ Ahead of time, place two cans of coconut
cream in the fridge overnight to separate
and harden.
♥ Bake the loaf and let it completely cool.

Cake layer:

♥ Preheat oven to 190°C/170°C/gas 5.
♥ Grease a loaf pan with coconut oil.
♥ In a small bowl, combine coconut oil and
stevia. Set aside.
♥ In a large bowl, whisk the salt, eggs, vanilla
extract, and almond extract.
♥ Whisk the coconut oil mixture into the
egg mixture.
♥ Whisk in the coconut flour, making sure it is
completely combined.
♥ Stir in the mashed bananas.

♥ Pour the batter into the pan.
♥ Cover with foil and bake for 40 minutes.
♥ Remove the foil and cook for another 10 to
15 minutes or until the top browns.
♥ Let it cool completely.

Coconut cream:

♥ Do not shake the can. Scoop out the coconut
cream that has hardened in your can of
coconut cream. You will be left with about
half a can. Leave the coconut water behind.
♥ Place the coconut cream in a bowl, add the
stevia and vanilla, and whip.
♥ Slice the cake loaf into 2.5cm layers. Spoon
some of the coconut cream into the bottom
of the serving cup, place a cake layer on top
and then cover with more cream. Slice the
strawberries and add. Layer to your desire.

Top Tip: I prefer to use canned coconut cream for this recipe — it's much easier to work with and whip!

Index